Blown Away
Seeds on the Winds of War

Ted Baverstock

First Published 2013

by Gallo-Romano Media

www.gallo-romano.co.uk

ISBN-10: 1492782513

ISBN-13: 978-1492782513

Blown Away

Seeds on the Winds of War

Published by Gallo-Romano Media

copyright 2013 Ted Baverstock

The right of Ted Baverstock to be identified as the author of this book has been asserted by him in accordance with the Copyright, Designs and Patents Act 1988.

Gallo-Romano Media is committed to publishing works of quality and integrity. In that spirit we are proud to offer this book to our readers, however the story, the experiences and the words are the author's alone.

All rights reserved. No part of this book may be reproduced or transmitted in any form or by any means, electronic or mechanical, including photocopying, recording or any information storage and retrieval system, without prior written permission of the Author. Your support of author's rights is appreciated.

DEDICATION

I would like to dedicate this book to my wonderful wife Jean who helped me unstintingly with the early drafts of this book. My life with her represents, without any doubt, the best thing that has ever happened to me. I also wish to thank my daughters, Suzie for drawing the narrative of the book together with numerous supporting photographs and Jenny for her initiative in pursuing sources of possible publication to a successful conclusion

I also wish to express my gratitude to Jill and Bob for their invaluable assistance and advice in publishing my story.

CONTENTS

	Preface	i
1	Introduction	1
2	Arrival	Pg 3
3	Old Farm	Pg 11
4	Springtime	Pg 25
5	Cattle	Pg 30
6	The Bull	Pg 40
7	Jack Exon	Pg 42
8	Horses	Pg 46
9	Water	Pg 56
10	Haircutting and the Amateur Village Barber	Pg 60
11	The Village Church and Religion	Pg 64
12	The Major	Pg 74
13	Dogs	Pg 82
14	Haymaking	Pg 87
15	Smoking	Pg 94
16	Shops	Pg 98
17	Butcher Durston	Pg 103
18	Cuckoo	Pg 105

19	Monty Tratt	Pg 106
20	Miss Vile-Strangways	Pg 108
21	Poultry	Pg 112
22	The Outing	Pg 115
23	Harvest	Pg 124
24	Cider	Pg 129
25	Free Fruit	Pg 132
26	Autumn/Winter	Pg 134
27	Girls	Pg 139
28	War in Shapwick	Pg 144
29	Threshing	Pg 156
30	Roaming	Pg 160
31	Village Elementary Education	Pg 168
32	Epilogue	Pg 194
33	Glossary	Pg 203

PREFACE

I hope that any who should read this story will accept that it is to the best of my recollection (unless attributed to others) and is written with gratitude, respect and affection to the Stevens family and their relatives. I have tried to tell of things that happened or were heard or seen by me, but if anything I have written should cause offence, I am sorry as that was not my intent. My aim is primarily that this story is for my children and other family members to read should they be interested and I trust this record will not be seen as egotistical on my part. Those others with experience of farming in the 1940s and onwards who may happen to read this, may find some inaccuracies in what follows (minor I hope!) for which I apologise. However, it is an attempt to record how I saw village life and how things were done at a small Somerset farm in those days.

1 Evacuation poster. Artist Dudley S Cowes

1 INTRODUCTION

Little did I realise at the time but my arrival in Somerset was to prove a contrast to what my life had been hitherto and was an entirely new experience influencing my outlook thereafter. Firstly, I must pay tribute to the Stevens family upon whom two other evacuees from London and I were thrust. It must have been difficult for them to receive us child strangers into the very heart of their family without any foreknowledge of who we were or what we were like. Though my thanks are due to the whole family, I must thank Mr. Herbert Stevens for his kindness and the interest he took in me. Most of all, I must thank Mrs. Alice Stevens for looking after my every day needs and keeping my behaviour under reasonable control. This must have been very difficult for her as not only did she have close involvement with me each day but in my final year I became much too cheeky to her, something that I have since deeply regretted. I realised soon after I had left what a debt of gratitude was owed. Later, I apologised to her to which she replied, "Well Ted, perhaps I was a bit too strict with you", a remark that touched me. I am so pleased to say that we became friends and the family has since welcomed me and mine on visits over the intervening years. Perhaps like some other evacuees, I became a bit disturbed from being away from my real family for so long, even though they came to see me at least once each year whenever possible. When my mum and dad occasionally visited, they too were always and generously received by Mr. and Mrs. Stevens and refused any payment offered by my father. They were also as generous when my sisters came to see me on short stays.

2 My family (Minnie, Mum and Dad) with Norman, me and Sid Witherington on a visit to the farm with Mr Steven's car

This new life introduced me into a community where many members still spoke using some terms that, to me, came from the King James Bible. "Thee, thou, thy, art, wert", were quite common terms among a sprinkling of other words of local dialect like "gurt" for great and "youm" for you are. Sadly, this lovely speech seems to have almost disappeared as have much of the rich speech burr and the sound of "s" pronounced as a "z". Among the villagers were many interesting individuals and characters that I have never forgotten.

The life that I led on a small farm involved me closely with a number of domestic and farm animals, their habits and needs. In and around the village, the wide range of wild life was also fascinating, as were many of the trees and plants. The seasons too also contrasted so much with those of town life, with haymaking and harvest being highlights of each year.

Please note that some names have been changed to spare the feelings of any individuals or their relatives.

2 ARRIVAL

It was the bleating of sheep that gently roused me from sleep. Through half-closed eyes I became aware of sunlight streaming through curtains lacing a large window. Drowsily, my mind attempted to recognise unfamiliar things with a growing awareness of the huge bed in which I lay so cosily. As my consciousness cleared I knew that this was not home and drowsily recalled the events of the previous evening. After the long and tiring day of travel from London, my recollections were scant. There was the arrival at this house of strangers who had welcomed Frank Crann, my fellow evacuee and me, and the hot meal we ate before we went early to bed. I now took stock of my surroundings. The bed was truly enormous. It was an ancient four-poster; its columns were of heavy, carved, blackened timber, with a massive headboard and wooden canopy. The feather mattress upon which I lay was so plump and soft that my weight formed a trench where I lay in blissful warmth.

As I relaxed again and drifted to the edge of sleep my mind played on the events of the day before. It was Friday 1st, September 1939, a day that was so much different to all others. With the threat of war with Germany looming, Mum and Dad had decided that I should be evacuated to a safe place away from Dagenham, Essex, on the edge of London where they, my sisters Minnie, Rosemary and me all lived. The government had made preparations for this evacuation and so on that morning when I went to school I carried a pillowcase containing a change of underclothes, shirt, socks, soap, towel, etc, and some food with my gas mask in its cardboard box hung by a string from my neck. In my jacket lapel was tied a label with my name and address.

School assembly was held in the playground that morning and those like me who were similarly laden and to be evacuated stood in our class groups while our teacher took a roll call. We were then shepherded in double file through streets that we knew well, past our homes where mothers waved to us from their front doors to board an electric train at Becontree station. Soon we were on our way to central London to the Great Western Railway terminus at Paddington. After another roll call we were bundled aboard a waiting steam train. None of us boys from Dawson Junior School knew the significance of the journey we were about to undertake or where we were bound. Though my recollection of the journey is now vague I do remember the initial excitement and our rough and tumble as the main line train got under way. Our noisy chatter filled the carriage compartments as we scrambled over the upholstery. It wasn't long before we made an early start on our packed lunches experiencing the novelty of our travel with little supervision. We felt as though we were on an outing with the school for a few days. Thus any fears and doubts that we otherwise may have had were allayed as we gradually subsided into boredom and relative quietness as the train sped along.

After many hours of constantly changing scenery past unknown towns, villages and green landscapes we arrived at Bridgwater in Somerset. Mustered by our teachers into our school classes and roll called again, we carried our kit through the streets past terraced homes built of vivid red brick. From the doors of these women and children watched as we passed. Almost before we knew it we were aboard a bus waiting at the River Parrett Bridge and bowling along out of the town and into the countryside through fields and over low hills. About thirty minutes later we disembarked at a grey stone, foursquare building at Ashcott which we later learnt was the village hall.

Assembled again with our luggage, we entered the hall and spread ourselves about the place on chairs and floor. After yet another roll call, names were called out and gradually boys were collected singly or in twos and sometimes threes by total strangers, mostly women, and taken away. My usual Dagenham friends had not taken part in this exodus so on the spur of the moment a classmate, Frank Crann, and I decided to stay together if we could. After a long wait he and I were introduced to a Mrs. Bird and with our bundles set upon her bicycle, we walked together the mile or so to her home at Pedwell.

3 Norman, Ted and Frank Crann

As I stirred from my sleepy reverie, so Frank who lay beside me awoke. Exclaiming at our new surroundings we were at once out of bed and at the window. Breathing the fresh autumnal air we viewed an orchard fronting the house where it stood on the flank of a hill with the broad expanse of Sedgemoor beyond. Mrs. Bird then entered the room, greeted us warmly and pouring water from a washstand ewer into a bowl, bid us wash and come down to breakfast. In a trice, washed and dressed and fairly tidy we were seated at table with her two children, Eileen aged about twelve and Ken about nine. The shyness of our first meeting the evening before briefly returned but we were soon chatting away like old friends. Mrs. Bird told Frank and me that we were with her only briefly. That afternoon she said, we would go to Ashcott to the house of her brother Herbert Stevens with whom we were to be billeted. He and his family were returning from holiday that day and until the time came, we were to play in and around her house.

The rest of that morning was spent in a scramble of exploration of parts of the house, some outbuildings and grounds. A partly furnished summerhouse (in reality a clean chicken shed with good headroom) was a private world for Eileen and Ken that we were allowed to enter. We visitors were shown all sorts of interesting things including a wind-up gramophone with a horn. Ken put a record on but instead of winding the handle he pushed the record around with his finger. A garbled sound of music came from the horn and then the main spring of the machine broke there and then. As its music groaned to a halt Ken looked momentarily shocked but no comment was made as we turned to other things.

4 The Stevens Family circa 1934

After a mid-day meal we were taken to our new home to meet Mr. Stevens, his wife Alice and their son Norman who was aged eleven. Mr. Stevens was a butcher by trade and worked for a local Ashcott farmer (Mr. Cousen) who also ran a butchery business supplying home-killed produce. The detached house forming our new home was pleasant with a rear garden of fruit and vegetables. Once again we had a friendly welcome and were shown to our room and leaving our belongings there, we went downstairs to be with our hosts.

The next day being the 3rd of September, we all gathered at 11am. to listen to a radio broadcast by the Prime Minister, Neville Chamberlain. War had been declared on Germany. My dad had told me that war was a terrible thing and what really frightened me now was the thought that he would have to go off to fight and would be killed. I burst into tears.

Our new home was pleasantly spacious, though smaller than the one we had left and situated in a quiet part of the village but within the sound of farmyard cattle. It too stood halfway up the south-facing flank of a hill, with a view from our bedroom window over the lower parts of the village and also Sedgemoor. On some autumnal mornings, extensive mists above which, a conical hill protruded made the moor mysterious. On days that would be fine, the mist would disperse except that part of it at the hill base. As the air warmed, the mist rose in an encircling ring giving it a curious collared look until dispersing at the summit.

Though Frank and I had arrived uninvited in the Stevens' household as a result of the pending war, we were accepted by them and also by their relatives and friends. We were both the objects of curiosity as well as friendly amusement mostly, perhaps, because of our cockney accents. For our part, we viewed our new acquaintances with interest, even though their Somersetshire accents often confounded us at first.

One day, Norman showed us how to lure wasps into a trap. He baited a jam jar with a mixture of jam and water, covered the jar top with paper held in place with an elastic band and pierced the paper with a small hole. Placing the jar on a sill in the garden, wasps were soon lured by its sweet scent. They entered the hole, fed on the mixture but could not escape and eventually drowned when they fell into the liquid. It was very effective and we felt protected from the stings we might otherwise have suffered.

Fronting the house was a lane. Opposite was a narrow grass verge at the foot of a stone wall. Here one evening, Norman showed us a wonder of nature as the evening shadows fell. Deep within the grass were several glow worms showing their greenish light. We gathered a few and took them in matchboxes into the house and later to our bedroom. When in bed, we were interested to see their glow when under the bedclothes where they stayed when we fell asleep. The next morning they were gone, no doubt squashed as we turned in our sleep.

There was also a black cat that was part of the household. This was the most elusive one I ever knew and haunted a lean-to building where split fire-logs and other miscellaneous items were kept. When we entered this building the cat regarded us balefully from far recesses and was ready to flee if we approached; so it was not be petted. It had its food there and earned its keep as it did duty as a mouse hunter. Norman also had a pet white rabbit, the first one of its kind that Frank and I had ever seen, kept in a hutch in the garden.

Frank and I attended Ashcott village school with all of the other evacuees and the village children. It stood partly on a high bank and was of redbrick with large windows. We were there for only a few weeks so I do not recall much about it. Norman had attended this school but having passed his Eleven Plus examinations was to attend Elmhurst Grammar School in Street about four miles away.

The village had many interesting places to see with a small shop by a tiny green where stood a large oak. Some farmyards were situated in the heart of the village though Frank and I did not have access to them. Some evacuees were lucky enough to live with farmers and so were in close contact with cattle, etc. Incidents occurred where some got into trouble, not so much from devilment or accident but more out of ignorance of country ways. Sliding down haystacks was unacceptable and that was soon made clear. Another one that was talked about in shocked tones by the adults during teatime one day was through a mistaken kindness to calves that had been weaned from their mothers. Some boys had watched them being fed from pails with a mixture of milk and bran and decided to give them some water. Having given them one lot they found the calves would drink more and more. Having given several pails full the thirst of these animals seemed insatiable. Luckily the boys lost interest in this after a while and stopped. When the farmer found this out he was horrified as watering them in this way caused them to "blow" or have very distended stomachs a condition that could kill them. Though not involved, that was our first farming lesson. Later, Ashcott though a larger village than Shapwick, seemed less interesting to me than its neighbour. This was probably because whilst there I had not the ready access to farms and open country that I would eventually experience when at Shapwick later.

The most interesting place to visit was the smithy where there always was some activity going on. Within its gloomy depths huge bellows were worked by hand, the gloom being suddenly lit by the flare of the forge as air was blasted into its hot coals. Heavy tools hung in rows. Stacks of iron bars, rods and heaps of scrap margined the floor. The anvil and the blacksmiths' faces gleamed in the light of the forge fire against a general sootiness. The smithy's sounds varied from the soft burr of men's voices or the occasional hoof stamp of a patiently waiting horse, to the clamour of struck metal as an item of farm machinery was mended or a horse shoe was shaped. Here we got our first close-up of really large horses.

Perhaps the most spectacular sights and sounds were from a scorched hoof as a new red-hot shoe was applied as a first fitting. A loud hissing arose as the rim of the hoof began to melt and clouds of acrid smoke enveloped both smith and horse. After other adjustments and fittings, the red-hot shoe held by iron tongs was plunged into a tank of cold water, causing hissing and bubbling as it cooled. With the hoof set on the peak of a metal tripod, the shoe was then nailed into place. The smith then lowered the hoof to the floor by grasping shaggy hair around the hock. As spectators to these events, we were not very welcome because of our meddling fingers but were tolerated at the door provided we did not get in the way of anyone.

One of the regular features of my new life was the need each week to write a letter home. These first efforts were daunting and required considerable encouragement and prompting before a sufficiency of words were written. It was always a thrill to get a letter from Mum and Dad but the initial replies were a particular thrill because they were the first real letters addressed to me by way of the GPO (General Post Office). Until then, the nearest communications that were addressed to me were reminders for the return of books from our local public library in Dagenham. At times I had deliberately kept the book at home beyond its return date merely for the pleasure of receiving my very own mail. It wasn't long before Mum had realised what I was up to and though amused, put a stop to it.

I particularly remember visiting a friend of the Stevens' family who lived a short walk away at the top of the village. She was a widow and Norman was a favourite of hers. We took tea with her that afternoon after which she asked each of us boys in turn to perform a song or recitation. Norman and I did so and then it was Franks turn. Being a Roman Catholic, he said he would sing a song called, "God Bless our Pope" and reverentially did so. When he finished there was a stunned silence in the room for several seconds and then another subject was embarked upon. I did not think much of it at the time but the silence that had occurred remained at the back of my mind. It was later that I realised that I lived in a strongly protestant community and Catholics were regarded as being odd to say the least.

3 OLD FARM

After a few weeks living at Ashcott, we three boys were overjoyed to be told we would be moving permanently to Old Farm in Shapwick about three miles away. Though Frank and I had settled down happily with our new friends in their home, the thought of living on a farm was enthralling. We already knew a little of the farm comprising of thirty-six acres, as we had visited once or twice to meet Granny Moxey (Ada Moxey, the mother of Norman's mum) and Uncle Jack Doyle, Granny's brother. As Mr. Stevens was now to run Old Farm, he gave up his full time job as a butcher, changing to a work arrangement of only Thursdays of each week. His work included a meat delivery round to surrounding villages by the use of a small van, an arrangement that fitted in with the morning and evening milking of his own cows that day.

So, one Saturday morning, we three boys were told to walk to Old Farm to await the arrival of the adults later. In the afternoon they arrived with a horse-drawn wagon laden with their furniture and goods. Old Farmhouse stood centrally in a large orchard, comprising mostly of apple trees but also two walnut trees of immense size, with barns and outbuildings on its western edge. A stream also bisected the ground in the muddy margins of which cows often stood as they chewed their cud. I was fascinated to see that a number of wild rabbits lived there in warrens under the orchard hedges and Frank and I attempted to catch them but, of course, without success.

5 Shapwick village (circa 1900)

A part of the farmhouse was very old with a later extension containing more rooms than the latter including a dairy and a washhouse. Its mediaeval part contained a large kitchen flagged with large randomly shaped stone slabs on which stood several items of furniture, all strongly built and heavy including three settles; two small ones in an inglenook and a large high-backed one at the dining table. There was also a large built-in cupboard that was more like a small room. Between the inglenook and this stood a large high desk where Granny sometimes wrote whilst standing. She used a heavy pen to write which it was said was made from some metal from a Great War gun. A window set in the thick wall looked out onto the orchard. The kitchen was the focal point of daily household activities where all meals were taken. Off it was a large walk-in pantry and near that was a door that hid a narrow stairway leading to two upper bedrooms where Granny and Uncle Jack slept.

6 Mum, Minnie and me in front of Old Farm

7 With Mum outside cottages in the centre of the village

Another room in the house that was always busily occupied each day was the washhouse. Here each Monday morning, the laundry was done at a brick built copper in a corner. It also heated water for our weekly bath on Friday evenings. These were taken in a tin bath carried in from where it hung on a wall hook outside the back door. It was set before the inglenook fire in the winter and in the spacious dairy in the summer and filled by a bucket from the copper. Being the youngest, I always had my bath last in the same water as previously used by Norman and Frank. In another corner of the washhouse we boys washed our dirty faces, hands and knees at the old hand-pump using cold water in a baler set on a strong metal grid over an iron trough. Soft water for laundry and personal washing came from tanks and butts outside, filled by gutters and down-pipes that collected rainwater from the roof. We mostly used this water and in the winter, broke ice to get it from a butt. The freshness of this startled us out of sleepiness when we came from our beds in the mornings. The iron water pump linked to a well beneath the washhouse stone floor, stood over the iron trough. The pump handle was large and "S" shaped with its end finished by a heavy iron knob. To work it, a technique had to be learned if water was to be quickly drawn. We soon discovered that a vigorous working of the handle with a sideways pressure would set it clanking, groaning and gulping hollowly. Three further thrusts got a trickle of water from the spout and then full spate after more thrusts. If plenty of water was needed, a rhythmical steady pumping caused a generous out-flow for as long as required, all accompanied by the clank of metal and the gurgling gush of water from the spout. The washhouse also included the back door leading into the vegetable garden.

The farmhouse was devoid of all of the now usual mains and drainage services. The inglenook range provided heat for the main cooked meals and room comfort. Breakfasts were cooked on a small portable paraffin stove set up on a bench in the dairy. A brass oil lamp set on the dining table illuminated the kitchen. Each evening it was lit by Granny and was like a pleasant, leisurely ceremony devised and acted out over many years. As dusk approached, the soft shuffle of her slippers on the stone floor was heard as she went to the dresser to check the lamp where it stood during the day. Having lit the double wicks and checking that they were neatly trimmed and not smoking, she replaced its glass chimney and adjusted the flame's brightness by turning two knurled wheels set above the lamp's paraffin tank. Then over the chimney was placed a glass globe etched with floral patterns. It was then carried to the dining table. As she hobbled across the room the lamplight cast huge dancing and heaving shadows from her small frail figure. It lit our evening meals, letter writing to home and board and other table games played by we three boys. There was a peaceful timelessness about the lamp lighting and its pale yellow glow. It and the fire glow in the inglenook gave a sense of restful warmth and security to the room and those within it.

In the winters we saw ourselves to bed with the use of a candle set in a dish-like, enamelled metal, candleholder carried by Frank or myself. As he was almost two years our senior; Norman followed to bed a little later. Our bedroom was reached by stairs at the far end of the house furthermost from the warm kitchen. In the first few winter weeks at the farm this nightly journey daunted Frank and I. Walking down the length of the downstairs passage, the candle flame fluttered and we were frightened by the shadows as they leapt about us as they also did when we mounted the stairs. When we became used to it, we deliberately tried casting weird shadows ourselves. Once within the unheated bedroom (most bedrooms were thus in those days) we quickly undressed and slipped shivering into our pajamas. Before climbing into bed we arranged all of our street clothes on the bedcover in a line under which we would lie for extra warmth. The one who carried the candle snuffed it out when in bed and we would slip into sleep once our cold feet had warmed.

TED BAVERSTOCK

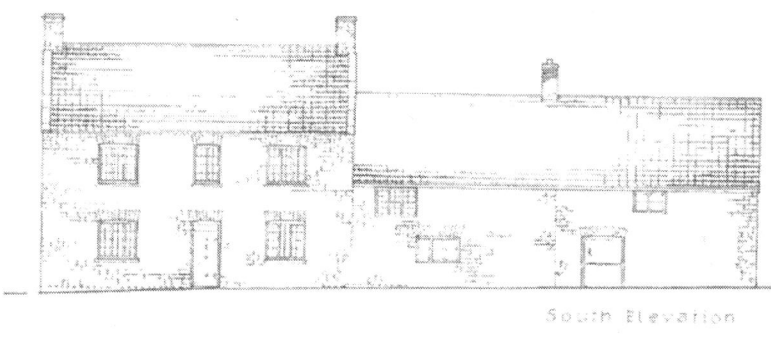

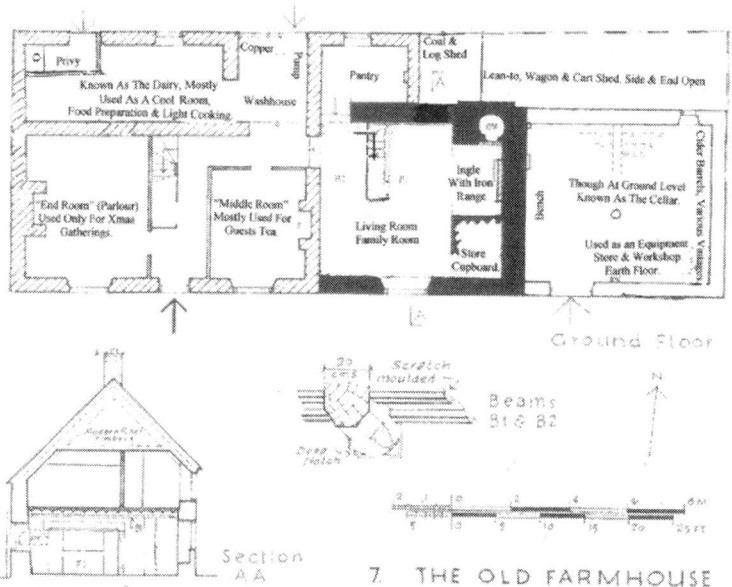

South Elevation

Ground Floor

Section AA

7. THE OLD FARMHOUSE

HISTORY. The presence of a large outhouse suggests a former farmhouse use and in 1785 there were 36 acres attached, the holding being part of the Main Manor. In 1839 George Biddlecombe leased it, and he and his brother farmed the newly formed 'Manor and New Farm'. The tithe apportionment description is 'house, garden and Stable. no 50'. This suggests that George was living there, the farmstead of Manor Farm being not yet built.

Tenants: 1660 (Church Rates) Mary Frew, widow; 1754 (Survey) Matthew Leaky; 1787 (Survey) William Leaky; 1839 (TA) George Biddlecombe; 1877 (survey) called 'Kings' with 20 acres.

8 Plan of Old Farm - courtesy University of Bristol

Though the unheated lavatory was within the main house structure, to use it meant going out of the back door and walking to its entrance door at a corner of the house. It was flushed with a bucket of water that the user had to carry for the purpose. The nearby stream connected to it by an underground pipe then carried flushings away. It was unlit; the only light was through a hole, six inches diameter, cut high in the wooden door so a battery torch also had to be carried after dark. Within, the walls were whitewashed and the lavatory itself was a wooden "Thunder Box" where I often spent time sitting at my toilet singing at the top of my lungs or imitating a military band by voice and kicking the box with my heels to simulate drums. Not very sophisticated behaviour I have to admit! I had to tone down the fancier flights of musical virtuosity after complaints from Mrs. Stevens. Who could blame her? As was the case with most ordinary people in those days, toilet paper was merely newspaper torn into squares and hung on a nail driven into a wall or on a hook within convenient reach. This was what I was used to at home in Dagenham.

Inaccessible from within the house and next to the kitchen was a large room that had an access door from the orchard. This was called the cellar even though it was at ground level and I have since wondered if it once was a cow stall in olden times. Within were a large workbench, bits of lumber and a row of cider barrels containing various vintages. Above it was a hayloft but used only as an apple store. There were also two lean-to buildings to the rear and separate from the cellar, one being an open cart-house and the other a coal and log store. Many other arrangements and habits were all new to we two evacuees as were the other little incidents and insights of village life. They all marked the change from life in Dagenham and our introduction to the extended family and the farm. Our new life in Shapwick had begun.

9 Rear of Old farm (2001)

When we arrived, Granny Moxey was, I think, in her early seventies, small, white-haired and clothed in black save for a white wrap around apron. She was still very active in the lighter chores of the household. By way of contrast her brother sat silently near the inglenook for most of each day in his grandfather chair that was draped with a fine, heavy, red patterned horse blanket. He seemed strange to us children as he stared ahead, hands folded over the handle of a walking stick set on the floor and between his knees. His words were very few and made only in response to a question bellowed at him to overcome his deafness. Obviously, he had reached a stage of dementia (not that I knew it at the time) and after a week or two we took little notice of him though holding him in respect and some awe. However, one day he gave me a big surprise. Resting upright in a recess at the side of the fireplace was a single-barrelled shotgun. It was used by Mr. Stevens for hunting wild rabbits and was an object of great curiosity to Frank and me, though we were forbidden to touch it. Temptation was too much for me one day when Frank and I were alone with Uncle Jack who seemed far away in his thoughts. Without lifting the gun down, I turned it so that by half lying along the adjacent settle, I could look along its sights. Whilst engrossed in this, the old man suddenly let out a roar of disapproval that caused me to start as if the gun itself had gone off. Uncle Jack though it was a wonderful joke and set up a wheezy chuckle that went on for about five minutes. It took me just as long to get over my fright. I think that was the only time I saw him laugh but the incident made us think that he was not quite so out of touch with his surroundings as we had hitherto thought. Neither he nor we mentioned the matter to others and, in fact, it was the last and only time he ever communicated with me.

The household and farm had a routine within which we began to fit and life in the village also began to show a pattern. However, one morning when Frank and I were playing on the floor in the kitchen things suddenly changed. Uncle Jack got to his feet and plodded off to the outside privy. A few minutes later there was a horrified shout from Granny Moxey from the washhouse.

"Alice, Alice, come quick!" she called to her daughter.

We heard a flurry of activity and running feet as Mrs. Stevens hurried out of the backdoor. A few minutes later as we stood awestruck, the women carried Uncle Jack in helped by Granny's son-in-law, Jim, who happened to be passing in the lane at the time. They lay the old man on the floor and the women knelt beside him anxiously calling his name. A cushion was brought to rest his head and as they lifted it, Uncle Jack gave an almighty groan. It was the last sound he ever made and it frightened us lads. We had never before seen a person die. Granny Moxey later remarked,

"I did see Jack come along the path and I thought he did look bad (ill) and then he fell under the lavender bush and that was when I called for Alice".

Uncle Jack was put in his coffin and was placed in the end room that was seldom used except for large family gatherings. He was there for about one week. When we boys went to bed it meant passing near to that room and because our heads were full of ghost and other similar tales, we scurried fearfully past and up the stairs as quickly as possible. The death of Uncle Jack seemed to set a seal on the changes that had had lately taken place in the lives of the Stevens family's mode of life. In an unsaid way, it established Mr. Stevens as undisputed head of the household and thereafter it was he who sat at table in the grandfather chair with its fine horse blanket.

One morning when Frank and I were at breakfast in the kitchen we heard a cracked voice at the back door calling,

"Be you there, Alice?"

Then a conversation ensued between the two with the unknown voice giving out a frightening laughing cackle now and then. This was too much for our curiosity and Frank and I stole to the washhouse door and peeped to see who was making the noise. It was old Mrs. Exon who had come to collect a jug of milk. She was thin, small, bent and wore a black dress and white apron. We were even more scared when we saw her face as we thought that she was a witch. I know now that such a thought was silly and unfair to the old lady but she did, unfortunately in some ways, resemble the witch portrayed in the then recent Walt Disney film of "Snow-white and the Seven Dwarfs". Her calling at the back door became a regular feature and so we became used to her and worried no more. She was the mother of Jack Exon who we later got to know well when he worked odd hours with Mr. Stevens about Old Farm after his normal duties at Beerways Farm.

One very sad and unhappy thing occurred shortly after our arrival to live at the farm. Norman's pet white Angora rabbit was kept in its hutch on a grassy area in the orchard just a few feet from the garden gate. We passed it frequently during our play until one day when it was seen to be in distress. It was lying on its side gently gasping and so Mrs. Stevens was called to see what was wrong. As she held it she asked,

"When did you boys last feed it?"

A stunned silence followed and it was clear that between us we had not fed or watered it for two or three weeks. Mrs. Stevens angrily scolded us and sent one of us to get some milk. Forcing some between its lips a little trickled in but almost immediately, the rabbit's eyes glazed over and it was dead. This was a terrible thing made worse by the fact that within a few inches of the wire mesh of the hutch was an abundance of lush grass. We were all very ashamed.

After a few weeks, Frank and I discussed whether we should ask if we could call our new guardians, Auntie and Uncle. When we were in the kitchen we asked Mrs. Stevens if that was alright to which she said "No". We boys were sorry to hear that and it was never mentioned again. I already knew that I was not a proper family member but her response gave me a feeling of greater separateness and I think that Frank felt the same way. I later understood that with her son she needed to reserve her special and undiluted motherly love and family affection for him.

10 Alice Stevens circa 1952

In those early days Mrs. Stevens occasionally took us three boys on shopping visits by bus to Bridgwater where we sometimes visited a high-class tea-room called "James's". It was above a bakery and cake shop and was the like of which I had never entered nor dined in before. It was posh and genteel with silver cutlery, spotless tablecloths and napkins with waitresses in traditional black dress, white frilly apron and white frilly cap to serve our needs. The sandwiches were thinly sliced, crust-less and cut into triangles. The individual cakes were small, served on a glass stand and delicious. This was really the way to live and was a kind of haven unknown in Dagenham.

I sometimes had my haircut in the town at an old-fashioned barber's shop near the river Parrett. Here town and country men-folk not only had their hair cut but several also were shaved. This service fascinated me because the customer, gowned in a sheet, was tipped back in the barber's chair and his chin, cheeks and upper lip covered generously with a thick, soapy lather applied vigorously by the barber using a small brush. Interesting though that was it did not compare with what came next. The barber took up a wicked-looking cut-throat razor, stropped it on a leather strap to sharpen it more keenly and then proceeded to cut stubble of the customer's throat and chin. Next, the cheeks were shaved and finally the upper lip. The last bit I really enjoyed for the barber took hold of the customer's nose and gently pulled it creating a comic look to the face thereby getting clear access for shaving off the beginnings of a moustache. Between passes with the razor, whiskers and surplus lather was wiped off onto a square of old newspaper laid on the customer's shoulder. Finally all traces of soap were dried away with a towel. My only disappointment on these visits was that I never saw blood drawn!

Frank and I were totally innocent of the facts of life when we arrived in Somerset. Only a few days after our arrival at the farm and both just aged ten, we were at a corner of the orchard standing looking through a large hole in a hedge through which a cow had recently blundered into the adjacent lane. Staring up at us from its lower level was a group of evacuees who had been in the village several weeks ahead of us. They asked who we were and after we had replied one asked, "Do you know the difference between girls and boys?" I thought this was easy and I replied, "Girls have long hair and boys have short." This caused gales of laughter from our questioners who then explained things in basic terms. This confounded Frank and I who later discussed what we had been told and decided that it was so incredible it could not be true. A week or two later we were with the same boys driving a herd of cows that were also accompanied by a bull. After about one hundred yards of this, the bull suddenly mounted a cow and thus, what we had been told happened between males and females was startlingly revealed!

Life in the countryside either modified, or in some respects, totally changed the outlook of us London boys. The pace of life was slower; the people seemed calmer than were those in towns. We found that there was always something new to do or discover. This was particularly so should you be fortunate enough to live on a farm or have access to one. The very existence and abundance and variety of wildlife around us introduced us to a whole new chapter of experience. The local children showed us where nesting birds were and I for one was surprised to discover that wild birds had different eggs to those of chickens that we had for breakfast. Moreover, wild birds' eggs and indeed their nests could also identify different species. There was an abundance of these birds ranging from rooks, jackdaws, plovers, swifts, swallows, house-martins and many others.

The arrival of spring in 1940 outdid anything that we had known in our earlier years of changing seasons. Fields, banks and woodlands were ablaze with cowslips, primroses, cow-parsley, etc. To stand beneath the orchard's apple trees and look up into the branches full of scented blossom, humming with the sound of bees was sensational. Life seemed to take on a new urgency, encouraged by the sun, showers and warm breezes. Before the advent of selective weed-killers, hay meadows were well provided with a range of wild flowers and were alive with bees, grasshoppers (which we spent some time catching) and many other insects. Local people showed us many wild plants some being of particular interest to them for their beauty including a small, delicate quaking grass.

We did several small jobs about the farm all of which we were pleased to be involved in but with one exception. The only one we were made to do was to chop kindling wood for the kitchen range, the fire of which was lit very early each morning by Mr. Stevens before he went to milk the cows. This wood was drawn from a large heap of hedge trimmings and chopped on a block within the orchard just by the garden gate. With two of us working at it and chatting, it was an enjoyable evening chore after school. When Frank left in 1940 it became my sole responsibility and after a while I became bored with it and daydreamed as I worked taking a long time to do this small job. I think that this behaviour gained me the reputation of a slow coach that led to Norman giving me the ironic nickname of "Lightning". Thinking back it was a job that I should have done with better grace considering how well I was cared for but; I was a naughty child I suppose.

Some of the impromptu games that Bob Grogan, another fellow evacuee, and I played in and around the Old Farm barns had an element of excitement and risk. One was a trial of strength involving 1cwt sacks of cow cake. Together we hoisted a bag onto the top of the fodder bin and then one of us took it full weight on his shoulders and then as the other counted seconds to see who could last longest before giving up. There we stood at each turn grunting, straining with legs near buckling. Another involved the thirty foot ladder set against a hayrick. Climbing to its top I faced the rick putting my hands on the side rails and then the insides of my boots and performed a thrillingly rapid descent without using any rungs. The landing was without harm as I kept my knees bent but I did notice that the skin on each hand had been worn smooth, hot and shiny. For my next descent I faced away from the rick and to save wear on hands clutched a handful of hay in each as protection from friction. Because I faced outwards as I hit the ground I sprang forward and into a short run. This was the best technique and we enjoyed this game whenever we could.

The shotgun that I had first become acquainted with in the farmhouse inglenook later was kept propped in a corner of the main barn. Its availability was too big a temptation for us to resist. So this too became a plaything though fortunately without benefit of ammunition. The first thing we did with it before play was to make sure that it was unloaded even though our fantasies with it involved shooting Germans.

4 SPRINGTIME

As far back as I can remember, of all of the seasons I have always liked springtime the most. Of course I was aware of it back at home in Dagenham where we saw trees and plants freshening and blossoming and were given lessons about it at school. There we put horse chestnut twigs in water to watch the leaves and blossom develop. The changes in our garden at home and in the parks and streets were also clear to us. But the full glory of spring and its impact was revealed to me at Shapwick in 1940. It was far beyond anything I had known. The fields, trees and woodland floors had a wealth of successive blossom or at other times, blooms all at once. The first experience was when Mrs. Stevens took us to Loxley Woods to pick primroses so that Frank and I could send parcels of them home to our mothers. There were thousands of clumps of these in full bloom on the ground among last year's dead leaves. They were like large yellow cushions and I buried my face in one to breathe a delicious scent. Even to me, a rough and ready East End boy aged ten, they were beautiful. I sent a small parcel of them home but never knew in what condition they arrived.

11 Me pulling Sid Witherington in the orchard

The orchard in which Old Farm stood was also fabulous in springtime. Pastures were yellow with cowslips. We found that where bees had not visited, the blossom yielded sweet nectar. We pulled off individual flowers to sharply suck the base of each. Though it wasn't very much it was delicious. The season had urgency about it with every plant bursting into growth and every creature hurrying to feed a new family. The fast flow of water in streams, the warmer air and fresh breezes and sudden showers all added to the lush revival. This orchard was the scene of many of our boyish games. Cricket was a fairly regular choice in summer at which Norman was an expert. Frank and I soon discovered that when it was Norman's turn to bat he was very difficult to dislodge. By his play, he gave us several lessons as a batsman, knocking our bowling all over the orchard. Once I even tried to get him out by not bowling but by throwing the ball hard at the wicket but to no avail. That ball was knocked for six too. When at long last he was out, he took on bowling and within a minute or so, Frank and I were bowled out and Norman was back in the crease. I have to say that these experiences caused my interest in the game to wane and that has remained with me in later life!

Norman was good at football too and had honed his skills on the playing fields of his grammar school. He became adept at dribbling the ball to the extent he could flick it up causing me to inadvertently touch it with a hand. He then claimed "hand ball" and so won a free kick. Subsequently, I was caught this way so often that I had to play with my hands behind my back! The only other cricket game we played was not in the orchard but in Croft, Old Farm's hay meadow after haymaking. The game became notorious and involved about 14 boys both local and evacuees. It was progressing well when the ball was knocked over a hedge and into a small orchard. Local boy, Ernie Argent went to retrieve it and having picked it up came rushing back shrieking in pain. The ball had landed on the entrance to an underground wasp nest and a number of the angry insects had attacked him, several getting inside his shirt. There they stung him several times more until as he rolled in pain on the ground, we beat his shirt with our hands to kill them. He was in tears, which wasn't surprising as he had suffered dozens of stings to his face, arms and body. Poor Ernie!

Other wonders were the various birds, their nests and eggs that were to be seen. Norman introduced Frank and I to many, the first being a robin's nest in a niche in the wall of a small barn. The nest was beautifully made from hay, moss and horsehair with reddish brown eggs in its soft and delicate cup. The second nest was a wren's built into a slot overhead in a wooden door lintel of another barn. This was even more delicate with eggs not much larger than a pea with shells so fragile that they were translucent and coloured a soft shade of pinkish fawn. The wide variety of birds in the countryside intrigued us. Flocks of lapwings fed on newly ploughed arable land in winters, the colouring of their eggs laid on stony soil made them almost undetectable. Swifts, swallows and house martins abounded in the summer. The swallows congregated in their hundreds on overhead power cables in the autumn before flying south and was a sight to see. From their incessant chatter they seemed to be highly excited at the prospect of their journey. Suddenly they were gone until the following year. Swifts were among our favourites as they had a habit of flying in close formations, diving just above our heads and screaming as they passed. In fact, one swift came so close to me that it briefly fluttered though my hair.

We found an owl's nest in a hollow apple tree. Reaching in the access hole an adult bird flew suddenly up to the top of the hollow.

Its unexpected flight caused us to recoil. Then, further reaching brought a fat and wobbly chick into view. Replacing it, further rummaging revealed a white egg that was surprisingly spherical compared with other bird's eggs. At another time, at the foot of a horse chestnut tree, we found a number of owl pellets that we dismantled to reveal fur, tiny bones and beetles wing covers. One local boy came from his home by the old moat carrying a fledgling cuckoo he had stolen from it's foster parents nest. It was almost ready to fly. Its size was astonishing and it seemed unconcerned from being handled. What I found striking was the hawk-like look and horizontally striped breast the bird had. I now fear that having been taken before it was fully mature it would not have survived.

We became fairly skilled amateur ornithologists and admired the many other birds that we saw. Gaining a good recognition of their eggs and nest construction we could identify which eggs, nests and nestlings were those of specific birds. We were allowed to make collections of eggs but only by taking only one from a nest and not having more than one of each egg in a collection. Some nests were always inaccessible like rooks and heron but many others were in easy reach in hedges and trees. Others like pheasant, partridge and lark nested on the ground.

By climbing the pigeonholes within the dovecote in the grounds of Shapwick House we were able to inspect jackdaw nests at close range as these birds had ousted all pigeons. One tree that I climbed had unusually good access by its many branches. At its very top was a magpie nest abandoned after the nestlings had flown but still in good condition. The fact that it had twigs to provide domed shelter for a brood within was a surprise. This tree was the only one that I could climb to its full height and be able to pop my head out of its crown to view the surrounding country.

Jackdaws were abundant in and around the village, as were rooks. Each autumn, swirling rackety flocks of the latter raided the Old Farm's orchard walnut trees to carry off the ripe nuts from the highest branches. Each successful bird flew off with a nut to eat it somewhere safe. But occasionally through an insecure hold, a nut would fall from the rook that then immediately returned for another try. Here and there in the hedgerows of outlying fields some young walnut trees grew as testament to a dropped nut from a raid years earlier. The rooks were wary birds not least because, as a deterrent,

Mr. Stevens sometimes shot a few, one at a time during separate raids. At the sound of a shot the whole flock, less the victim, rose in a cacophony of calls to circle at a safe distance. This deterrent was short-lived, as the rooks were soon back and this despite their downed brothers and sisters being strung on display in a row on a lower branch as if on a gibbet.

5 CATTLE

When Mr. Stevens took over the farm from Uncle Jack it had only five cows and one calf. The herd was a mixed bunch, variously coloured, ranging from the young to the old. All were individually named. Herfie was the oldest at thirteen years and then there was Bluey, Trixie, the lovely Pansy, and Blackie. Pansy was a kind of beauty queen among cows. She had shapely, perfectly balanced horns and her black and white Friesian markings were nicely proportioned. She was without doubt, not only the best of the herd but also one of the finest cows in the village. She had a huge udder and gave milk plentifully. Her other main attribute was her calm and gentle manner that also showed in her clear, long-lashed eyes. Herfie lacked good looks and was ancient. As a Hereford, she had the white face of her breed and horns that turned down and inwards. If her horns had grown a few inches longer, they would have poked her eyes out. They were reminiscent of the handles of a racing bicycle but there was no speed about Herfie as she ambled along. Bluey and Trixie were sisters and Roans, the one had a distinctly blue-grey look as her name implied, and the other was a reddish-beige that was almost pink. Trixie was the herd boss but did not over impose herself on the other cows but sometimes had trouble in keeping Blackie controlled. As the youngest, Blackie may still have had the impetuosity of youth but her aggression was mostly because of her highly-strung nature. She was always challenging the others except Trixie. Blackie would also shake her horns at us boys but a raised stick would cause her to turn away so she never took matters further.

12 Frank, me and Norman with Herfie who died soon after

It was about a month after we moved to the farm that Herfie died in her sleep one night. When the news was broken at breakfast, I was the subject of some chafing from the household. This was because my eyes filled with tears and my lips trembled. I suppose that I was the only one to regard the animals as members of the family rather than economic necessities. Shortly after this the herd was extended by two purchases. One of these was Cherry, a younger sister to Blackie and of the same colour and temperament. The other was Snowball, all white of course and a daughter of Trixie. This small herd eventually expanded to eighteen or twenty. Later after Mr Stevens retired, Norman, the son of the house with his wife Dulcie, farmed at New Farm. Together they developed a first class herd of about eighty cows with twenty-five follower heifers and calves. This was a wonderful achievement from small beginnings that earned the respect of other Shapwick farmers and villagers alike. Frank and I eventually laughed about our first encounter with the herd when we first came to the farm. As we walked to them across the field, so a week-old bull calf took it into its head to jump and cavort. Thinking we were being attacked, Frank and I ran for our lives to, and over a nearby fence. The look Norman gave us seemed to say he thought we were each soft in the head.

In the cooler months of the year another pleasurable job for us boys was bringing the cows back to their stalls each evening from outlying fields to remain in their stalls overnight. Farmers called, "How, how, how," to their cattle at such times causing them to respond by ambling to the field gate and to start the way home. We soon learnt this technique which saved a lot of walking about rounding them up. It was interesting to note that they mostly took a well-trodden and worn track to the gate and they walked mostly in single file along its winding way. By being involved with them on a daily basis meant that we got to know them well and they us. As far as Frank and I were concerned our confidence and interest in them grew rapidly. We undertook several other enjoyable, simple winter tasks for them including mucking out their stalls, cleaning dried mud from mangolds taken from store before shredding them on a hand operated machine for fodder. Chaff cutting and cattle cake crushing was also similarly done. These foodstuffs were then allocated to the manger for each beast. They particularly liked the cake and now and then a bossy cow would try to steal another's supply only for us to drive her off.

When Frank left in 1940, Bob Grogan, my special mate and me often went together to collect the cows. Mr. Stevens had told us to drive them home quietly and this we did. Sometimes a few cows would trot off ahead of the others, presumably with the thought of cow-cake awaiting them in their mangers but mostly they behaved. When the road verges were lush with spring grass we allowed them to graze quietly as we wended our way. This suited Bob and me very well as we frequently played with a stream by the roadside, damming it to make the water back up to form a pond only then bomb the dam with stones to destroy it and make the water surge downstream. We sometimes were so absorbed in this that the cows were strung out along the road for about a ½ mile. We only took them to pasture after morning milking at weekends as Mr. Stevens did it himself on school days. There was an exception to this when I had to take the cows to the Limekiln fields one March morning in 1943. Mrs. Stevens had given birth to a daughter (Marjorie) and Mr. Stevens wished to visit them at Butleigh Hospital that morning. Even though it was a school day I was told to drive the cows about three quarters of a mile to pasture. It was a slow job and as I ran back to the village I knew that I would be late for school. Upon arrival I was taken to task by the teacher and told to explain my lateness. I thought it very unfair as it was my only lateness ever and as I answered I was near to tears. When I mentioned the birth, the teacher's attitude changed though not the tone of her voice and I was ordered sharply to my desk but without punishment.

The well-being of the herd was of paramount importance so it was carefully tended, well fed and quietly handled. The continuation of the herd was also vital and the birth of a succession of calves throughout the year ensured this and likewise sustained a fairly even milk yield from the cows. The birth of calves was always awaited with great interest but sometimes led to complications that kept Mr. Stevens and the veterinarian surgeon up all night. In themselves, the calves were always a delight to see but were taken from their mothers after two or three weeks. All heifer calves were kept with others of around the same age, in separate stalls by the paddock to grow on to maturity to develop the herd further. However, the bull calves, almost without exception, faced an altogether unhappier fate. They went to market on the same day as they left their mothers. Both mothers and calves would be very distressed at these partings and set up an almost constant lowing for each other over three or four days. Then as hope of reunion was lost or memory faded each animal settled down to a separate existence.

Another enjoyable daily task for we boys was to feed these calves from buckets containing a mixture of bran and milk until they were weaned. A calf newly parted from mother was wary of our approach at first but hunger quickly overcame its initial reluctance to feed. Such a calf would not understand how to drink from a bucket so in the traditional way, our fingers were offered as substitute teats. As they were readily sucked, the animal was induced to lower its head into the bucket and draw up the liquid around our fingers. Despite getting our fingers sticky with saliva, it was a pleasant task and evacuee friends would gladly join us to feed the calves in this way. Care had to be taken as calves had a tendency to butt the bucket when feeding, just as they butt the udder when suckling a cow. A firm hold on the bucket was required to prevent the contents from being sent flying. When the calves got used to the routine, each mealtime as we approached they would chorus a greeting as they looked over the half-door of their stall. After a cow calved, the first two or three days of her milk were very nutritious and must have contained other elements to give the newborn calf a good start. There was always a surplus of this milk after the young one had fed but because of its special nature, the milk could not be sent for human consumption. This milk, known as colostrum, is very thick and bright yellow. So that it was not wasted we boys fed it to the other calves in the usual way.

The cattle had to be treated for ailments and infestations that meant a need for a watchful eye for their condition. Most problems were minor and easily treated, one being cattle ticks. These unpleasant parasites were pale-grey and oval and could be found in the hide of cows. A nastier one were the worm-like warble-fly larvae that burrowed into the cow hides raising prominent bumps and damaging the hide making it less valuable for leather. Other sicknesses meant a visit from the vet. Now and then a cow sported evidence of the treatment given, such as a poultice contained in a sacking bag tied around its foot. This poultice was to draw infection from within the cloven part of the hoof but while it was worn, the cow looked as though it suffered from gout. Liquid medicine was sometimes needed. This required the sick cow to be tied at the head in a stall and as one man forced her snout up anther poured the medicine down her throat. When I saw this technique done the cow was alarmed at first but she then relaxed. As the bottle was withdrawn, the cow gave it an appreciative lick to show that she wanted more. At times an unavoidable disaster occurred no matter how carefully treatment was administered. The lovely Pansy, pregnant with twin calves had birthing complications and both were stillborn. Two or three days later Pansy also died of a condition, mysterious to me, called milk fever. It was all very sad.

As calves grew to heifers, they were evaluated with a view to involvement in improving the stock to a stage where it qualified as pedigree. Part of this involved the completion of a white card bearing the outline of a cow's head full-faced and the left and right views of the cow. Each heifer was allocated one of these cards onto which the black markings of its hide were added and sent off to an adjudicating organisation. If the animal was well marked with a balance between black and white and with a reasonable ancestry, it was accepted and was a first step in the right direction for the pedigree objective. Over the years, Mr. Stevens with close support from Norman and Dulcie

Stevens, painstakingly developed the herd in this way to top quality.

Now and then another cow was purchased to expand the herd, usually from Bridgwater market. It was interesting to see the new arrival's introduction to the herd. As it was delivered to a field to graze, the present herd raised their heads to stare at the newcomer. She was apprehensive for a while in her new surroundings grazing at a distance from the rest who ignored her. She stayed separate and alone for a few days and then took courage to move closer to the others that carefully watched her as they too grazed. At this time, the boss cow was always the first to come forward. Boss and newcomer stood facing each other at about two and a half yards apart. Gradually each stretched their necks out in a tentative inspection of the other, all the while sniffing loudly. Noses would gradually get closer and then with necks at full stretch, noses touched in a very damp kind of kiss. In an instant both cows flinched, lurching nervously away only to repeat the procedure until curiosity was satisfied. The new cow then went though the same introductions intermittently in turn with the rest of the herd, it all taking several hours. After a few threats and minor skirmishes, a day or two passed and the newcomer was accepted and could be seen content and in close company with the rest.

We also took interest in the cattle on other farms, especially the pedigree Friesian herd owned by the lady of the manor. This herd at Church Farm was under the control of a bailiff and comprised about sixty head and a magnificent bull. The bull was of massive physique being kept in a heavily barred enclosure in the farmyard and was only brought out to breed. When a few of us lads knew that one of his lady friends was being brought to him, we used the gate to the farmyard where he was kept as a perch from which to view the action. All bulls are potentially dangerous but we were unsure whether this one was, as he seemed placid enough in his pen. When brought out for nuptials, the man leading him had to hurry, not to get out of harm's way but to keep pace with the eager bull. The huge animal always made a beeline for the cow and without any preliminaries or by your leave, would mount her. Within about five seconds the encounter was over and both animals were led quietly away.

There was one famous episode with this bull that took a little longer than usual. The object of its lust this time was a heifer. The maiden waited as the bull came out at his usual brisk trot. Without even inquiring her name, he suddenly placed his full weight upon her hindquarters. Being totally inexperienced, the heifer collapsed lying spread-eagled on the ground. It was all very undignified which was not made less by our roars of laughter as we fell helplessly off of the gate. For a moment, the bull wondered where his ladylove had gone but seeing her predicament, he gallantly stepped aside. Looking decidedly startled, up the heifer scrambled and seeing the bull had not lost his ardour, then braced herself successfully for his assault.

Fees earned by a bull for breeding could provide a significant income for a farm especially if the pedigree of the bull was good. So that advantageous genetic attributes were acquired in a herd, a farmer sought the best bulls in the district to service his cows. One young bull of high pedigree was owned by Butcher Durston. He had reared the animal on his farm from a yearling and having just reached maturity, it was ready to breed. One of Old Farm's cows was to be his first experience. Dawned the happy day and the cow was presented to the bull. Up he rose, rampant and eager. Disaster! The cow was tall and the bull was short. After several attempts and as many failures, the engagement was broken off with the parties dispersing to their respective farms. Fees are not paid for only a good try at breeding by the bull.

Bulls should never be trusted though some breeds seem placid by inclination and the Herefords are to me prime examples of this tendency but it was easy to give a bull the wrong impression. I was once running down a lane and past a field containing a herd and a bull. As I ran, I found the bull snorting loudly, was keeping pace with me on the field side of a barbed wire fence, looking for an opening. The stupid creature mistook my haste for flight and was out to finish me off. I need hardly add that I took myself onto the lane, which was deep and ran on as unobtrusively as possible and mostly out of his sight to safety.

When cows were out to summer pasture, both morning and evening milking was done in the field where they grazed. Tethered in turn to a post in a hedge the other cows waited patiently nearby. One regular daily task was to supply water to them in the absence of a field pond. This was done by filling five or six empty milk churns at the farmyard and with the use of Jack the pony and his cart, hauling them to where needed. A man could lift one full churn unaided but it took two boys to do the same. We liked driving the pony with these loads and then tipping the water into the makeshift troughs in the fields.

One of the talents that Mr. Stevens had was water divining. As the fields at the Limekiln were without natural surface water he began a search for it with a hazel rod or wand cut from a hedge. The wand was "V" shaped and gripping its ends in his fists with palms uppermost he walked the ground with it held horizontally and pointed forward at shoulder height. Near the field boundary next to the road the wand gave a twitch and then began to curve irresistibly downwards despite his grip tightening in an attempt to stop it. Noting the position, during the next day or so he dug a pit and found water. Though it supplemented the supplies that we hauled it was not a prolific source so only partly eased our work. Of course, the return journey with the cart included churns containing the milk yield.

One day whilst the milking was being done I went for a walk to one of the Limekiln fields where I knew were a lot of rabbits, one of which I hoped to catch. As I entered the field, I saw there were about twenty of them including several young. Seeing me the adults became alert so I dropped on all fours and began to crawl quietly to them supposing that they would then see me as just another four-footed animal. This didn't fool them except for one of the juniors. As I edged quietly near it we regarded each other with interest as it kept nibbling. Then I pounced, and with squeaks of fright it panicked and ran to-and-fro under me enabling me to grab it. I was delighted and hurried to Mr. Stevens to show him my trophy. He was mildly interested and I was surprised how calm the rabbit became the longer that I held it. After petting it for a while I took it back to where I had caught it and let it go. Even then it did not rush away.

During one of the return journeys from milking, Mr. Stevens and I were in the cart with him driving. He was in a hurry and with a whack on the pony's rear with a stick, urged him to speed up. We were moving at a fast pace as we came down a slight incline close to the village when suddenly Jack slipped and fell down. Mr. Stevens and I were flung forward and finished hanging, heads downwards over the front board of the cart. It was all very quick but collecting our wits we were soon out of the cart and onto the road. "Sit on his head so he can't get up so he doesn't entangle in the harness", I was told and did so whilst the harness was released. By this time a man from a nearby cottage had come to help. When free of the harness, Jack was helped to his feet looking a bit shaken. Hands were run over his legs to check that they were not badly injured and after a few minutes he was re-hitched to the cart and then driven quietly home. So much for being in a hurry!

Watching the cows being milked by hand, I found that it was inadvisable to look too closely as with a flick of a wrist, the milker could direct a squirt of milk into my eye as a joke. I longed to be allowed to do some milking myself and though I asked on several occasions during the first years of my stay, it wasn't until 1943 that Mr. Stevens relented and allowed me to try. Milking by hand for an hour or more requires strength and stamina in a man or woman. Though I would not be expected to milk for more than fifteen to twenty minutes I think that he had weighed up the physical strength in my wrists and hands and for a long time found them wanting. For my first try, he wisely did not give me a young cow to start with but the oldest, Trixie. He did not want his best cows spoilt in any way and old Trixie was quiet and tolerant to a novice's attempts. Sitting on a traditional three-legged stool I did my stint and when finished Mr. Stevens took my place to see how much I had failed to extract. It was a very small amount and he was satisfied saying that it was important to strip the remaining drops as any left would tend to reduce prematurely the cow's output. So from then on I milked a couple of cows whenever I went with him to the fields and I was delighted to be able to help.

Mr. Stevens was expert at handling his herd and, with only occasional help from other men, mostly did the milking by himself both morning and evening of each day. Sometimes a cow was very fidgety causing him to shout at her in a threatening voice that usually brought the desired effect. Should the animal kick the bucket or try to move away he sometimes stood and whacked its flank with the stool. That immediately stopped any nonsense. There was one astonishing event during an evening milking in a field when he lost his temper with a difficult cow. It was the only time that I had seen him really angry. Putting the stool and bucket to one side, he went to the head of the beast. Taking its horns in both hands, he gave the head a wrench to one side and over she went onto her side on the ground. I think that he was as surprised as I was amazed. The cow scrambled up to stand, stock-still, and milking resumed with no further trouble. I was very impressed at what I had seen. Though nothing was said afterwards between us nor ever mentioned at home, I could not resist boasting to my friends about the strength of Mr. Stevens.

Every now and then the herd would be kept in the orchard to graze. Mr. Stevens said that when the apple crop was nearing maturity there was a slight risk to a cow from it reaching up to gain a low hanging apple. It could get lodged whole in its throat and then choke. I could appreciate this happening but never saw it occur. They did do some other things that caused concern. Once, a cow stretched over the garden hedge to begin to eat a tablecloth spread to dry on a gooseberry bush. Granny Moxey was just in time to rescue the cloth after only a little chewing.

Other incidents were not so much for the cow's safety but the protection of vegetable garden crops. They broke into the vegetable garden once or twice and having discovered the cabbages and Brussels sprouts feasted briefly before being driven off. One raid caught them in the mint bed. That evening, our nightcap of fresh milk was distinctly mint-flavoured. As cabbages and sprouts were harvested in the winter so several stumps with their coarser leaves on were spread for the cattle in the orchard. They were eager for these but it amused me to see them chewing on these as though on a bizarre cigar.

6 THE BULL

After I had left for home in Dagenham, I was told the following story concerning how this herd grew and its quality improved over the years. Mr. Stevens and Norman acquired their own pedigree bull that as it neared maturity became a handsome creature. One day, Mr. Stevens was taking it to pasture at Croft along Back Lane by leading it quietly using a short pole linked to its nose ring. They walked along quietly when Mr. Stevens stumbled to lie flat on the road. The bull stopped and regarded Mr. Stevens interestedly as he began to rise. As he did so the bull gave him a friendly nudge with his snout sufficient to send Mr. Stevens down again. In an instant, the bull knew he was the stronger and his true nature then emerged. Down on its knees went the bull, his horns thrusting in an attempt to gore. Shouting in alarm and squirming away, Mr. Stevens gained some limited sanctuary at the base of the hedge with the bull on its knees attempting to come after him. Luckily, Mr. Argent a neighbour living in a cottage close by heard the shouts for help and standing at his garden gate, shouted and waved his coat causing the bull to divert to him. So, Mr. Stevens made his escape and apart from being a bit shaken and with a few bruises was alright.

The bull was very dangerous from that day on and was confined to a heavily barred spacious pen and stall and never let out. Cows visiting for breeding purposes were always let into him instead. Thereafter, it was only possible to get close to the bull by standing in a heavily barred lobby that formed part of the enclosure. Such closeness had the bull glaring, snorting, lashing his tail and rolling his bloodshot eyes. He was formidable and would have delighted to kill somebody, though he did not know it, he did obtain a sort of revenge on humans. Being the nature of the species, he was not in the least particular where he defecated. Often it would spatter the walls of his stall. Just as often he would soil himself by leaning against these walls and flicking his tail in the mess. Though he was kept clean by being washed down by hose he would soil himself between washes. Any visitors viewing him from the safe area at such times would suddenly be aware that patterns on their clothes were acquiring additional colouring. As the bull lashed his tail, greenish brown streaks and polka dots would be imprinted on suits and dresses.

7 JACK EXON

Jack Exon was a cider drinker. So was a high proportion of other men of the village but Jack had his own approach to the subject. Basically a shy man, he seemed most at ease in the company of men and boys. He seemed to have no social life other than through his work as a farm labourer at Beerways Farm or in the company of Mr. Stevens for whom he did some casual work. He lived with his elderly mother, the same lady who frightened Frank and I so when she called at the Old Farm door for a jug of milk when we first came to live at Shapwick. She was well into her seventies and, strangely, called her son "Father". She kept house for them both but his married sister kept an eye on their general well being, doing all of their day to day shopping.

As a bachelor, Jack was painfully shy of women except for those in his immediate family. During the time that I knew him he was in his early forties. Should he find himself in the presence of a woman other than family he was reduced to bashful silence or was tongue-tied when speaking. If drawn into conversation with her he only managed to mumble replies. On these occasions, his normally florid face took on an even deeper red. He was illiterate (perhaps dyslexia) and those who had attended school with him as children said that he struggled with lessons. Even so, as far as money matters were concerned, he had his wits about him and was not to be tricked or short changed. Though he earned a lowly wage it was rumoured that he was well off. This was based on the fact that he spent little money.

He was a highly skilled farm worker and could turn his hand to any job the farm required. He was hardworking and strong for though he stood a little more than five feet tall, his back was broad. He also carried a big firm-looking belly cultivated by a hearty appetite and cider. His work on the farm seemed to be from 6 a.m. to 6 p.m. each weekday and only a half-day on most Saturdays. As Old Farm was immediately opposite his front door he did not have to walk far when required. He also had to take his turn with milking at weekends on a rota with his workmates. He got to-and-fro to work and home on an old, large framed bicycle. The ricks that he thatched could be told apart from the work of others as his trade mark was a tuft of straw at both junctions of its ridge and hips. His other hobbies apart from cider drinking were cultivating vegetables in his cottage garden and on dry evenings he stood looking over his front garden hedge to engage passers-by in conversation, mostly us boys. As I have mentioned, he also did evening and some weekend casual work for Mr. Stevens.

Jack was amused by the antics that the village boys and evacuees got up to and tolerated our impudence good-humouredly. When engaging us in conversation he inevitably started by saying in his broad Somerset dialect, "Wherrart thee gwan?" (where are you going?) He also regarded evacuees as having arrived almost from another planet and clearly thought that we had all come from a heavily polluted and densely smoky environment, though it must be admitted a much smokier one compared to that of Shapwick. This was obvious from his other regular question, "Be thee down frum the smoak, Lunnon?" (Are you down from the smoke, London?). Having said this kind of thing, his eyes screwed up in amusement and he chuckled away, his big belly bobbing up and down as it rested in his garden hedge. One thing that Jack had learned well was how to swear and his sentences were regularly punctuated with the ripest examples.

The only things that drove Jack from his leisure time vantage point at the hedge were: mealtimes; the appearance of a woman who was likely to enquire after his mother; and, because he never attended church, the approach of the vicar or Major Royle, especially the latter. These sudden retreats had a lot to do with shyness, but as he swore so prolifically I think that he was afraid he might have a lack of control over his tongue in polite company.

Jack was always dressed the same. Once each year he paid a visit to Bridgwater Fair, being the only occasion that he left the village or its immediate environs. Whilst in the town he bought a beige, three-piece twill suit, a pair of heavy corduroy trousers, two collar-less shirts and a pair of heavy boots. Upon arrival home, he discarded the identical items of clothing that he had worn all year, brought out identical items purchased the previous year for regular daily wear and placed his new clothing in his wardrobe. An old pair of leather gaiters, that never seemed to wear out, completed his ensemble. As the fair was held in September of each year, Jack looked unusually smart for a period immediately following though never with a collar for his shirt. This smartness was fairly short-lived because hedging started in early winter so the front of his replacement waistcoat quickly became shredded, resultant from his belly being thrust among hawthorns and brambles when cutting and laying hedges. One's attention was drawn to the tattered condition of this garment when Jack occasionally consulted his turnip watch kept in one of its tattered pockets.

Jack kept a hogshead of cider at home from which he helped himself as he felt the need, which was frequent. This supply was handsomely supplemented by free access to Old Farm's cider cellar for which he had permission to visit as often as he liked. I never saw Jack very drunk though he was frequently a little smilingly unsteady on his feet. At times he visited the cellar when we boys were about. There he stood after drawing a pint, quaffing it with one arm draped lovingly over its source, a huge barrel. Being basically honest he would have paid his visit for just the one drink. Knowing his weakness, we boys often said, "Bet you couldn't drink another one without taking breath". Jack with the flavour lingering in his mouth, struggled not to weaken and then proved us wrong. We then challenged him for a second time and after a show of resistance, he proved us wrong again and so it went on. Jack thoroughly enjoyed these contests and we were highly amused not least because his complexion took on a deeper shade of scarlet. At the end, Jack would unsteadily but still smiling, wend his homeward way across the orchard.

He was the only person that I ever saw who could drink by pouring liquid straight down his throat without the swallowing reflex. This was best demonstrated by a quart of cider in a bottle. "Bet you can't drink that straight down without stopping", we would say. Up went the bottle; Jack gazed skywards as its neck met his lips and then his Adam's apple disengaged. Non-stop, the straw-coloured cider flooded down his throat until the bottle was drained without hindrance. Jack then smiled in triumph and a few minutes later was even more affable than usual.

Jack was a likeable man and I look back on my times in his company with a kind of affection. I hope that I haven't made him seem soft in the head because he certainly was not. He was just an ordinary man and a character, with simple everyday needs and a few mild, human faults.

8 HORSES

The first time I saw Jack the pony was when Norman, Frank and I walked the two miles from Ashcott to Shapwick on a visit to Old Farm. The farm's orchard was laden with its autumn crop of rosy cider apples. There he stood, old and black-coated, still as a statue, drowsing in the heat of the day.. The pony had already been the subject of some talk among us. Having been all of one week in a rural environment, as he came into view I drew on a wealth of experience of horses. This came from what I had seen when watching Tom Mix and Buck Jones cowboy films at Saturday "tuppeny rush" children's cinema shows and from observing horses pulling milk or coal carts. I airily said,

"You can see that he's been ridden a lot."

"Why is that?" asked Norman.

"Well," I continued, "you can tell by the dip in his back. That's there because of the weight of people that he has carried."

Norman's face took on a look of incredulity and he said

"No-one has ever ridden old Jack. He's the wildest pony for miles around and has always been the same."

With me silenced for my stupidity, Frank and I then regarded Jack with a mixture of admiration and respect.

When we moved to Old Farm, I got to know him better and for his reputation to be confirmed. At the time Jack was the sole means of haulage and transport for the farm, being used to pull a small cart or a trap. With Granny and Uncle now in old age the pony and cart was used to go to and from the cows in distant fields for milking.

Adults, usually Mr. Stevens, were the only people who could catch Jack. His anger and aggression seemed reserved only for boys. In his harness and hitched to the shafts of the cart, Jack seemed to accept that he was under the control of whoever drove the cart. For a horse of around thirty years he was still able to set about his work at a brisk trot, despite a swollen knee. When out of harness and grazing in the orchard he was still compliant with adults but with boys he was a demon. This I can only put down to the probability of some ill treatment by lads in his earlier life. The stories we heard of him when he was young, lashing out, biting and plunging when being brought on hind legs from his stable certainly impressed us.

13 With Mum, Mr Stevens and Jack the pony

One day, Mr. Stevens was in a hurry to finish some task or other and needing the pony and cart told us boys to take a rope halter, catch Jack and bring him to the cart. Off we went to where he peacefully cropped the grass. Approaching quietly we called to him encouragingly and softly in a fair imitation of Mr. Stevens. Jack raised his head and fixed us with a stare. When we were about four or five yards from him and moving slowly and cautiously, his eyes rolled to show gleaming whites. With ears laid back, up he reared and at us he came. The three of us scattered and with a backward glance I saw that he was concentrating on me. Terror filled my mind as I ran to the nearest apple tree in the blind hope of some form of refuge, maybe in its branches. Being small and the branches high there was no hope for me by that escape. So around the trunk I ran with Jack close behind. Around and around we went until I realised that he could not gain on me any more because the length of his body caused him to turn in a much wider circle around the trunk than was necessary for myself. In fact at times I was catching him up. This merry-go-round began to slow and eventually stopped. There was I breathless on one side of the trunk with Jack snorting and eyeing me malevolently from the other.

This stalemate restored the confidence of my companions and to some extent my own. In an attempt to rescue me they approached waving arms and shouting. Biding his time until they were as near as they dared to come, Jack once more set off this time heading for Frank. Norman feeling safe, laughingly and inattentively slowed to a trot. With a sudden change of direction Jack was behind him, neck stretched and great brown stained teeth bared and reaching for the nape of Norman's neck only inches away. Together, Frank and I shrieked a warning and saw Norman glimpse the situation. With a desperate spurt he gained the safety of a tree trunk with only inches to spare. White faced, it was his turn on the merry-go-round that I had just experienced. After a while Jack appeared to lose interest. With Norman still by the safety of the trunk we gradually and quietly edged away as the pony began to crop the grass again though keeping an eye on us all the while. We then returned to Mr. Stevens to confess our failure and without any rebuke to us, he crossed the orchard took Jack by the forelock and walked him quietly to the cart shed. Jack seemed to be thinking, "I only deal with men so beware lads because I'm out to get you".

As you can tell, Jack was never to be trusted by us boys. Try as we might, he would not be friendly to us. When he was stabled we sometimes offered him some precious linseed cow cake that we knew he liked. With his head over the half door he condescended to take with his lips the knobs of cake from our flattened palms. After several offerings of this delicacy he appeared content and friendly. As soon as we tried to stroke him however, flat back went his ears, his eyes rolled and showing their whites wildly, his head rose ready to bite. When Mr. Stevens acquired an Austin Seven car and small trailer for the milking trips, Jack lived in a state of semi retirement compared to the life of other horses in the village. They had to contend with the annual slog of ploughing, harrowing, seeding, raking, haymaking and harvest as well as other work. Then his leisure increased further sometime during 1941 when Mr. Stevens bought a carthorse mare, Pleasant. She was much bigger than Jack and in stark contrast with him, she was of a gentle nature. She did the heavier work of hauling muck in a tumbrel for spreading on meadows in late winter and hauling wagons of hay or wheat sheaves from the fields at harvest.

14 Pleasant the carthorse

His companion mare became the great love of Jack the pony's life. The contrast between them was considerable. She, a large chestnut with a white blaze down her nose and a white "milk splash" on a hindquarter, he, a medium height gelding pony totally black save for a white star on his forehead. Her arrival ended Jack's loneliness. When not at work, they kept close company, contentedly grazing or standing together contemplatively. On summer days they stood close together but facing opposite ways so that as they flicked their tails they kept annoying flies from each other's faces. These days of quiet contentment continued untrammelled until the following summer. Until then neither the mare nor pony seemed dominant in their relationship though Pleasant dwarfed Jack physically. Another carthorse, Prince, was then borrowed from another farm for haymaking. On a lovely summers evening, Pleasant and Jack were released from work into the orchard to graze. Prince followed shortly after and as he entered the orchard he saw the others on the far side. Ears pricked forward and at a brisk trot, he approached them calling with a low whinny. The others raised their heads sharply to watch the intruder. After a moment, Jack ran at Prince, rolled his eyes to show the whites, stretched out his neck and flashed his teeth. Prince, who after all only wanted to be friends, was surprised at this and stopped short, only to then veer aside as Jack wheeled about and brought his hind legs up in a vicious kick. Because of his age and a certain stiffness, Jack's kick was not what it once must have been so Prince was able to sidestep in time. Though Jack was small, his spirit was big and he harassed the horse to a distance. Only then did Jack return to his ladylove who had watched the whole process with interest. Then both settled down to graze again. Over the week or two that Prince was with us he realised that his presence was only just tolerated by Jack. Though he eventually moved nearer when grazing, Prince remained at a respectful distance from the others for the rest of his stay.

Though I aspired to be a horseman, opportunities to ride were relatively few because most village horses were of the heavy draught type. Mary Marsh, the bailiff's daughter had a lively chestnut pony that could give an exhilarating gallop. The pony was tolerant and allowed us to leapfrog onto its back from the rear and then take three or four of us on a walking ride in this way. It was great fun but the trouble was that her dad did not encourage riders other than Mary so these games were in his absence and with Mary's permission. The rides were bareback but I once had a ride on this animal on an autumn evening as shadows were falling. Mary let each of us boys in turn to ride to the end of the field and back at a canter. It was a terrific thrill to race along, then turn and race back. But being bareback I had difficulty in staying on and as we slowed to a halt I suffered the indignity of almost slipping off. I saved myself from falling by hanging upside down under the pony's neck with my feet around its shoulders. It was not a spectacle to impress my friends. Even so, these were the only rides that I had during the whole of my time in the village with the benefit of a proper bridle.

All other riding was also bareback, sometimes with just a sack to serve as a saddle. Moreover, there was always only a rope halter with a webbing head-stall to guide the horse and I found it difficult to remain mounted when the horse I was riding moved briskly. The most worrying ride I had was on completion of some haymaking on the moors, by Mr. Stevens and Mr. Jennings, on a field about five miles from the village. The men were to ride home on an old stripped down but powerful Ford car that served as a small but fast, makeshift tractor. Norman and I were told to ride Pleasant and a pony home. Norman had first choice and unsurprisingly chose the pony. The animal belonged to Mr. Jennings. This farmer worked in co-operation with Mr. Stevens with mutual benefit for their individual farms. I was left with Pleasant. Each animal wore a sack as a makeshift saddle and each had a rope halter to serve as a rein. The pony was just the right size for Norman but Pleasant was several sizes too big for me. The mare towered above me especially as I was a small boy for my age, so I had to be lifted onto her back. There I sat with my legs widely splayed across her bulk. The men saw us on our way with the pony leading at a walk before they climbed aboard the Ford to quickly overtake us and then disappear from sight.

After walking quietly for a while, we boys agreed that a little trot would not be amiss. Urging both horses vocally and with a few thumps in their ribs with our heels, both duly obliged. The pony was no problem to Norman. However, the long striding Pleasant caused me to jiggle about insecurely on her back as she loped along because my legs were too short to get a good grip to her flanks. The pony being swifter soon increased her lead and when Pleasant noticed this she accelerated in an attempt to keep up. This jolted me further upwards so that there was about six inches between her back and my rear at each stride. Uncomfortable though this violent bouncing up and down felt, it was nothing to the jarring I got when she decided to slow down. It was then that my rise and fall became seriously out of synchronization with hers so that when I was coming down she was coming up. The painful buffeting and bruising my bottom and another part of me received caused me to yell to Norman to stop.

Slowing his pony, he allowed us to catch up when we once more resumed a leisurely walk whilst I reflected on the folly that the idea of trotting had been.

After about a half mile, Norman got bored with our pace and trotted quietly away at a canter. Thankfully, Pleasant did not notice their departure, that is, until they were about two hundred yards ahead. Totally disregarding my shouts of "Whoa", she decided on an attempt to catch them up. This second performance of bruising to my rear end was just as agonising as the first but sustained for a longer time. Norman was oblivious to my shouts of anguish and he and the pony continued at a brisk pace. I, on my lofty perch had given up all hope of steering or restraining my steed. Letting her have her way, I clutched both the halter rope and her mane in desperation to stay on. After much too long a time Norman and pony disappeared around a bend and Pleasant slackened her pace. As she slowed to a walk there was more violent jarring till she was once more ambling along. Oh, bliss!

It was a warm sunny day and the mare had worked up some sweat. I was damp too but it wasn't only from my own exertions and panic. I noticed that the sack on which I sat was distinctly damp from horse sweat. By now we were passing a few wayside cottages. Opposite to them and one field away were two or three horses. Noticing her own kind, Pleasant decided that she would like to join them. Turning onto the verge she leaned over the hedge, ears pricked, to test the hedge by trying to walk through it. There was an ominous sound of twigs and branches snapping and I hauled on the rope with all of my strength but only managed to turn her head slightly. I hauled and shouted getting a bit hysterical but the crackling continued. Suddenly a woman appeared from a cottage. She ran to us and, grasping the halter guided us back onto the road just before the hedge gave way. I thanked the lady for her help and we went on our way again, me still straddling the horse but feeling humbled in my role as a rider.

After walking for about an hour we arrived at Old Farm's yard and Pleasant took several long draughts of water from a trough as I slid down her flank to the ground. As my feet touched down my legs collapsed under me. They had been splayed for so long they seemed incapable of coming together again and had momentarily lost their strength. Staggering up, the rubberiness in them eased but I was then aware of the sweatiness of my damp, short trousers. Not only that but I had acquired a distinctly sweaty, horsey smell and several stinging "saddle sores". Checking the sores later in my bedroom, I saw there were several glowing on my buttocks and down each leg. They took about two weeks to heal.

Jack was the only animal I knew that did not lie down to sleep. This habit was probably due to his having something wrong with a foreleg knee that was usually swollen. When in his stable, he slept standing with his hindquarters against a timber partition and his head drooping. He slept similarly when in the orchard but propped rearwards against a tree. One very wet day, I watched him from the farmhouse window as he stood in the pouring rain bored by the tedium of it all. After a few moments, his head began to droop and off he dozed. Having forgotten to back up to a tree this day, his rear gradually sank ground-wards. Just as it seemed he would sit down in an undignified way he woke up to recover his stance. Off he dozed again only for the process to be repeated several times and to my amusement.

Flatulence is a condition possessed in quantity by all horses, particularly if their diet is rich. Whilst driving a cart and standing in it holding the reins, other evacuees and I quickly learned to hold our breath when the horse raised its tail. Jack was at times a virtuoso performer in this respect and seemed occasionally to be especially impudent when his need was great. To cite an example of this, imagine a warm summer evening. It is nearly dark and I am in bed and settling to sleep with the bedroom windows wide open. Faintly in the distance, I hear Jack trotting. As he passes the house he is breaking wind. Not in a great burst but short bursts consistent with the movement of his hindquarters. These successive, short, raspberry sounds grew louder as he approached and fainter as he receded once more into the distance. Giggling sleepily to myself, I fall asleep. Jack often did this.

I did once see him off his feet enjoying the pleasure of rolling on his back. It was springtime and I think that the sunny, warm weather had stirred his blood. After much rolling about, he struggled to his feet and then shivered all over producing a cloud of hair from his coat that drifted away on the breeze. Considering he was black, this hair was surprisingly brown but of course, he was shedding his old winter coat.

I was told later after I had left the farm, that Jack lived to nearly forty. He had been fully pensioned off for a couple of years until his legs gave out. There was no alternative but to call in the knacker. As Mr. Stevens did not want him to leave alive in case he was maltreated he was shot humanely on the farm where he had lived for so many years. So that was the end of a spirited and at times wicked servant to the farm. Despite his faults I warily liked him and admired him for his spirit. I had a real affection for Pleasant though as I could rest my head against hers, stroke her neck and speak quietly too her as she stood peacefully.

One incident with Pleasant put Mr. Stevens in serious danger. He, the mare and I were in a field at the far end of the footpath leading from the vicarage where there was a small hayrick that was part of Old Farm's crop. The mare was harnessed to a small cart and Mr. Stevens was cutting hay from the stack and placing it onto the cart. He had almost finished when he suddenly slipped from the cartload to land trapped between the mare's hindquarters and the front of the cart. He just managed to keep his footing but the mare was startled by the suddenness of it all. Had it been a less placid horse than Pleasant it was likely that it would have lashed out its hind legs. It was clear that Mr. Stevens knew this because he called to her firmly to be still and then carefully lifted himself clear by heaving up with one hand on the mare's rear and the other on the cart. It was a close thing as he could have been badly injured if not killed from violent kicks. He and I said nothing about it but I could see that he was shaken.

Another horse I recall, I first saw as a foal with its mother in a small field next to the village hall that at one time served as our school. She was a brown carthorse and he a chestnut with a lighter mane. We boys watched the foal develop over several weeks from early unsteadiness to cavorting skittishness always keeping close to his mother. One day both had gone, taken back to Manor Farm. Some two years later about six of us boys were playing football on this farm's field among the cowpats. As our game flowed to-and-fro we were suddenly aware of a heavy drumming sound on the ground. As we looked we were rewarded with the sight of our foal friend. He was no longer the shy, slim creature we had known. Now, he was almost fully-grown and of superb physique. He was out for a gallop just for the thrill of being young and strong. Past he came at full stretch, his muscles rippling beneath his shining coat, his heavy hooves thudding the ground and sending up showers of clods. As he neared the boundary hedge he attempted a sharp about turn. In a slithering scramble of limbs, with mane and tail tossing, he only just kept his feet. An instant later he was off in the opposite direction passing close to us at a gallop and was soon out of sight. Though I never saw him again, the image of him that day has stayed vividly in my mind ever since. As a small boy and as a man now, that moment of display by the young horse represented the quintessence of youthful exuberance, physical strength and joy of living, all rolled into one.

9 WATER

Though not the wettest of the English counties, Somerset can fairly be described as damp. This is not merely due to its relatively high rainfall but also because of its many streams, rivers, marshes, dykes and ditches (called rhines) on the moors. Nowhere was this abundance of water more apparent than on these marshy moors (also called levels) about two or three miles north of the village. Glastonbury monks had drained them in the Middle Ages to form pasture. The network of drainage rhines were mostly set in a rectangular pattern. A larger level, Sedgemoor, lay a similar distance in the opposite direction and was similarly drained by the monks. With the winter rains the rhines on these moors brimmed over and the fields lay, usually for months, under great sheets of flood water. With the onset of spring the waters gradually receded to provide the summer pastures from which the name of Somerset is derived. Large areas of the moor to the north of Shapwick were devoted to the extraction of peat, much of it being used locally as domestic fuel. Some men of the village were employed cutting blocks of the sodden peat by hand. It seemed hard, back breaking work. These blocks were cut into slices and then wind and sun dried in conical, hollow stacks. Punts were used to convey peat from new workings across old flooded, worked out peat beds to collection points.

On the moor to the north of the village, one punt abandoned in a leaky state was found sunk in a rhine by about five of we lads. Heaving it from the water we upended it to drain and re-launched it. Using fencing poles we propelled it along for a short voyage. Our voyage lasted for about fifty yards before the punt sank as we abandoned ship just in time. Undaunted, we emptied it as before and in this way went up and down the waterway several times. It was just another adventure that brought us fun and laughter. It was hard work too. Later on we stole some bitumen from some road works to use to plug the leaks. It wasn't a success and the punt continued to regularly sink beneath us but we had some sport from it.

Though this peat cutting was a considerable local industry, most ground on the moors provided summer pasture and hay. There Mr. Stevens had a field or two in some years onto which heifers and dry cows were turned. Being in relatively lonely places, these cattle lost much of their regular contact with humans for several weeks. This caused them to become semi-wild, nervous and frisky when approached even galumphing about in an ungainly caper. Of course, they were kept under the watchful eye of Mr. Stevens who paid frequent visits to the edge of the field to check that all was well. Moreover, farmers and others on the moors also kept a helpful eye on other people's stock as acts of good neighbourliness. This was just as well as occasionally a message would come to a farmer that one of his animals was trapped in the mud of a rhine. This meant that an urgent visit to the scene for a rescue. Tying a rope around the animal's horns and pulling gently but steadily on it, either by a team of men, a horse or a tractor, the cow was hauled out. I often wondered how a cow felt after such an event. It must have had a crick in its neck for days after. Some never learnt from this experience and would get into trouble again.

The sense of wateriness was all pervading on these moors even in summer and I found that they had a strange, sour smell about them when I walked the fields. Trees and hedges were relatively few and were mostly willows, known locally as withies. These trees were the source of materials for other local industries of basket making, thatching spars, etc. Here in early summer, Mr. Stevens sometimes cut thatching for his hayricks and straw mows from the broad swathes of reed beds. He sometimes found a reed warbler's nest, abandoned after the brood had flown earlier. He brought some nests back to Old Farm for our interest taking pleasure from showing us its delicate structure, woven onto reed stems acting as stilts to keep it clear of water.

To us London boys, natural watercourses were mostly unfamiliar features with the exception of the river Thames or lakes in public parks. In and around Shapwick there was water galore. We spent hours of our free time exploring each pond, lake or stream and locating sources. We delighted in damming parts of minor streams for the pleasure of forming ponds from the backed-up water and afterwards watching the water surge away when we broke the dam. These moments satisfied all sorts of our schoolboy adventure fantasies that were usually set around fighting Germans or a gallant attack by us on the Spanish Armada. Imaginary explosions and cannon fire were imitated by noises we made and the cannon balls were stones thrown at twigs floating downstream in simulation of ships. This caused us much excitement and the Armada was defeated on several occasions. Most of this gave mild amusement to any adults who happened to walk by whilst we were so engaged but we usually played in this way undisturbed.

Not all of these events were warlike. There was an episode when we made miniature sailing clippers from flat pieces of wood, thin sticks for masts and sails from small paper squares. We raced these successfully in light breezes on "Greasy Pond" next to the village shop and were surprisingly realistic as they sped along leaving trails in the duckweed. This pond and the stream that flowed through the village were the nearest to home but we ranged far and wide to play with water. Sluices, weirs and lonely ponds or lakes were particularly fascinating. One "paradise" pond contained fine-grained clay, suitable for modelling. Tree trunks and gate posts surrounding it were soon ornamented with heads and masks formed from this medium until washed away by rain or cracked and crumbled by the sun. A small, flooded, stone quarry was a favourite place to visit where it lay among trees outside the village near Kent Farm. Its depths were a haven for many sorts of water creatures such as water boatmen, pond skaters and caddis flies. We also found a caddis flies larva case woven from tiny plant fragments like a tubular basket. As well as dragonflies, moorhens and coots, lizards were found among cracks in the stone margins. We tried frying moorhens eggs in an old saucepan found dumped in the water but in the absence of lard they always stuck to the its base so were not very easy to extract to eat. Other waterfowl were often in great numbers in the district. On moonlit nights in autumn or early winter, great skeins of geese were seen flying high above the village en route to the moors or more distant waters.

One spectacular sight to me was a heronry in the Icehouse Copse on rising ground near the moors. The copse was large and dense with several tall trees. At the very tops were numerous heron nests of long twigs built by generations of these wonderful birds. It was a remote and lonely place that added to the atmosphere created by the birds. As we stood under these trees gazing up, the herons flapped sedately high above to and from their nests. They also presented a slightly comic sight with their necks folded back and legs stretched out to the rear. They were rather awe-inspiring as they flew. Their cries, ungainly movements as they landed on nests to feed their young and the sharp clash of beaks conveyed to us an impression of the prehistoric.

One winter's day when testing the depth of a stream by stepping in I found that it was deeper than expected. I ended standing in it with the water filling my Wellington boots. Squelching out, I attempted to empty one of these by raising one leg in a forward kick. Water ran out and right up my leg only to make matters worse by wetting the seat of my short trousers. Arriving home snivelling, cold and soggy there was an adult, in the person of Mrs. Stevens, who was not amused by my watery antics who quite rightly, told me to take of my wet clothes and go to bed without any tea.

10 HAIRCUTTING AND THE AMATEUR VILLAGE BARBER

"Short back and sides" remained the standard haircut in those times presenting an opportunity to practice one of our playground tortures on each other. Unless the individual with the haircut was particularly formidable, one of us took a knob of coke from the school's fuel heap to then grab a victim and then rub it up the back of his scalp. You will know that coke has in its structure hundreds of small pores and as the stiff hair stubble entered these, it was painfully tugged by the piece of coke as it was rubbed upwards, much to the dismay of the victim. It was like adhesive plaster being slowly pulled from hairy skin but worse as I can vouch from personal experience.

Without combining it with a visit to Bridgwater paid for by an adult, obtaining a simple service such as a haircut could be a problem. The need could either be met by taking advantage of a bus trip to Street, (expensive for our pocket money), or a walk of around five miles there and the same back. In effect, it required a start from Old Farm at about 9 a.m. on a Saturday morning with the aim of arriving back before 1 p.m. that is if the queue in the barber's was not too long. When in reasonable funds, I caught a bus there but walked back saving some boot-leather, cash and energy. It was on one of these trips in a National bus with my friend Bob that the conductor treated us to an acrobatic display. When the bus got to Ashcott, all passengers alighted and we were alone with the conductor who engaged us in friendly chat. Then to our surprise, he gripped the parallel handrails attached to the ceiling of the bus and as we sped along, the vehicle rattling and jolting, he did a series of twists and loops mostly while hanging upside down. His grand finale was to hang by his feet from the rails trailing his arms on the floor. We were most impressed. The distance covered during the performance was about two miles. When the bus stopped at Walton to collect more passengers, our conductor friend went about his business as though nothing had happened except for his slightly reddened face and a wink in our direction.

Mr. Hooper, who lived in one of the terraced cottages at the village crossroads, saw an opportunity to corner the market in haircuts as far as male villagers were concerned. His qualifications were a wide experience in sheep shearing. As the haircut mostly required by men in those days was a "short back and sides", he only had to concentrate on that requirement ignoring such fancy styles like "a light trim" that might be sought by effete townies. Word got around that he had bought himself a pair of hand operated hair clippers and was available on dry evenings from 6 to 8p.m. before he went to the pub. His charge of sixpence-(two and a half new pence) per haircut undercut the barber in Street by threepence (one and a quarter new pence). When considering the matter, this and the fact that no fares or distant hikes were involved, clinched the business for him. His availability to cut hair on dry evenings only can be explained by his wife's refusal to allow it to be done in their home because of the mess she would have to clear up. Draped in an old bed sheet, customers sat on a kitchen chair on a paved area at the back of the cottage. I anticipated that this new service was a great blessing until, having reached a certain state of shagginess I paid him a visit. Sitting in the chair and hung about with the sheet, he took my head in a grip not unlike a rugby player grips the ball when running for a try. Thrusting the clippers against the back of my scalp he worked them hard upwards to a point about two inches above the level of my ears. As the clippers progressed they were pressed so hard that a small bow wave of my skin was forced up. Thus the haircut continued with me staring out from under Mr. Hooper's armpit, face contorted with pain. After about ten minutes of this agony he released his grip and surveyed his handiwork. If it wasn't windy, clippings littered his pavement and looking at the quantity I wondered how I now looked. He hardly spoke a word but if satisfied with the job he gave a grunt and then took up his scissors. If things were not right he attacked once more with the clippers. He was a bit uncertain in the use of scissors but chopped at the overhang of hair where the clippers had stopped and took just a little from the crown.

15 My haircut

Paying my sixpence at my first visit I left by his back gate ruefully rubbing my head wondering whether I had nicks in my skin and if so, how bad they were as the service did not include mirrors. As with all "short back and sides" styles, the hair stubble felt like stiff velvet when touched. Examining the results in a mirror later, I thought that all things considered it did not look too bad except for a fringe resembling the eaves of a hayrick encircling my skull where the clipping had stopped. Because the service was so close at hand other boys and a few men had haircuts by him in the first year. As his skill did not improve with time we boys began to complain to each other about the torture of it. Finally, we began to look upon the long walk to and from the barber at Street as only a small disadvantage. So, after about three haircuts each, Mr. Hooper's part-time barbering fell into disrepute and then disuse.

So, not having to walk to Street and the saving of boot leather was short lived. Because of a stupid prank of mine one day, this saving of leather was lost at a time when my boots had been newly repaired only the week before. A coal delivery lorry was parked outside the bakery and was about to be driven off when Bob and I reached it. Wanting to show off, I held onto the tailboard as the lorry moved and so I gained a sliding tow for about 25 yards, letting go before the speed was too great. Walking back to Bob I realised that my boots were unusually hot and lifting one to examine its sole, I was shocked to see that many of the new metal studs had been worn away as was about a third of the thickness of the leather. Its companion boot was no better and so the date for another repair bill for my parents came sooner than had been expected. Needless to say, I kept quiet about my foolishness.

11 THE VILLAGE CHURCH AND RELIGION

Shapwick's St. Mary's Church is a grey stone building and I think, Victorian. I have since understood that it replaced an ancient original church that stood away from the village in the direction of Beerway Farm. Within, it was rather Puritan plain but with some stained glass windows, a brass spread-eagle lectern and a few wall monuments. When a villager died, he or she was invariably buried in its churchyard. The funeral processions I had seen in Dagenham involved either a horse-drawn or limousine hearse. In Shapwick the coffin was placed on a bier, a kind of frame made of dark varnished wood set on four tall spoked wheels. Relatives of the dead person drew it through the village lanes to the church by pulling on a wooden "T" bar shaft with the other mourners following on foot. It was a simple and dignified procedure. Mr. Harry Barnett acted as undertaker and had a kind of monopoly on this because he had the business of village carpenter, joiner, wheelwright, builder, etc. He also made coffins.

In his spare time, Mr. Stevens was involved in several duties with the church. His activities went on quietly from year to year as a churchwarden, the captain of bell-ringers and sexton. With the small village population the need for burials was infrequent but when it arose he could be seen, often alone, digging a grave. I went with him on one or two occasions when he was engaged on this to see him short, stocky and strong, making light of his task. His tools were a spade, fork, shovel and pickaxe and as he took up one of these to begin he gave a spit on his hands to obtain a good grip. Under one of the huge spreading cedar trees in the churchyard was a spoil heap where surplus soil from graves was heaped. I was surprised to see tiny fragments of human bones scattered among the deposited earth. One day I helped a little with the back filling of a grave after the mourners had departed. With the grave partly filled the only help I could give was to assist in treading the loose earth within to compact it so that when finished, its mound did not sink below the general level as it settled later. One of the villagers was helping this day. Aged eighty years, Mr. Bartlett was in the grave treading with me as Mr. Stevens shovelled earth around our feet. I had the thought that if I stamped and jumped up and down my soil compaction would be more effective and started to do it. After a minute or two the old man said,

"I'd bide a bit quiet if I were thee, young-un, otherwise if thee keep that up e'll be up after thee."

Quietly amused, that remark caused me to revert to treading only.

Church bell ringing was suspended during the earlier years of the war, being reserved as a national warning should Germans have attempted to invade and, supposedly, in the event of BBC radio transmissions being knocked out by enemy action. The warning sound of bell ringing would be heard from city to town to village rather like the signals of hilltop beacons that were lit long ago to warn of the approach of the Spanish Armada. As the war situation eased in the later years so the resumption of bell ringing was allowed. The consensus in the village was that this revival was a good thing and I suppose gave the feeling among us that the tide of war was turning in our favour. A very much out-of-practice team of men, including Mr. Stevens as captain, assembled in the belfry one day. Norman and I were allowed to watch the bell-ringers at their task. We listened as the captain outlined mysterious instructions to the team including one called "Bob Major". After the ringing had started and continued, the captain gave a call at intervals to indicate change in the sequence that the bell ropes were pulled to give variations in the peals. We boys did not understand the finer points of this tradition but we could tell that some of what we were hearing was ragged due to lack of practice. During these practices one of our biggest thrills was to mount the spiral stair to the belfry where the different sized bells were hung. The clamour within this confined space as the bells swung was almost overpowering; seemingly giving a trembling density to the air that could be felt in lungs and through ones skin. Furthermore, the air felt as though it could be bitten. It was quite strange and fingers were quickly thrust into ears to lessen the din. To speak to each other was impossible even at the top of one's voice unless at very close range.

Eventually, a Sunday was nominated for the first full performance when it was thought that the practicing had reached a satisfactory stage. All went well at first with the sound of the peals tumbling down rhythmically. Then the clang of each bell started to closely follow the next, causing each bell in turn to be rung ever faster to keep ahead of the one preceding. In the end all bells were being loudly rung, virtually together with a sound like, THRANG, pause, THRANG, pause, THRANG, pause and so on. After a few minutes when recovery was hopeless, the ringers were called to a halt to resume at a steadier pace. Thereafter, bells on a Sunday were a regular feature with some mid-week practicing and the ringing became expert again. At New Year there was a virtuoso performance, or so I thought. Around midnight the bells sounded out but this time they were half muffled. The effect of this was that the peals sounded alternately; firstly in the normal way on one peal and then quietly on the second representing joy at the New Year and sadness at the departure of the old. I was very impressed.

As my parents never attended church services other than for weddings, funerals and christenings, as a child in Dagenham I knew nothing about them other than Sunday school. Being part of the Stevens' household I was expected to attend St. Mary's with them as they were regular worshippers and I readily complied. They habitually used the same pew in the church, as did the other parishioners in theirs. I liked singing the more rousing hymns and some of the psalms but the preaching by the vicar, The Rev. Seamer, bored me deeply. I often tried to follow his words but usually failed. Perhaps his sermons contained philosophical thoughts, but whatever they were about usually eluded me. It did not help that he had a sonorous and rather quiet voice. The pew was uncomfortable to sit on, and to stop my rear from becoming numb, I tended to fidget bringing a sharp reminder from Mrs. Stevens to be still. My companion Frank was a Roman Catholic and was forbidden to attend any church services other than those of his faith. When I attended church with the family he stayed at the farmhouse with Granny Moxey who was too old to walk to the church. This arrangement went on until two weeks before Frank left for his new school. On a Sunday Mrs. Stevens told Frank that he had to come with us to church. This shocked him but he came. When we entered the church and reached the aisle, he fell to his knees to face the altar and crossed himself. To me this was rather theatrical and I was amazed. As the service progressed he did more of these actions whilst in the pew still on his knees in a cringing, humble, posture. I think he felt that he had committed a great sin by being there. The following Sunday there was a repeat performance by him before he departed Shapwick forever.

I attended my first harvest festival in September of 1940. The harvests were good that year as the weather through spring and summer had mostly been fine and often glorious. Arriving for evensong with the family I was surprised to see the nave already filling. Moreover, the church was alive with flowers and the altar, flanked by wheat sheaves, was decked out with fruit, vegetables, loaves of bread and other tributes. It was very festive and so many people came, it was standing room only. This contrasted with the usual much smaller Sunday congregation when the pews were only half-filled. The traditional harvest hymns were sung; "Harvest Home", etc. As the multitude of voices was raised, the whole church was filled with sound from these hymns like I never knew before as many more baritones, than usual, joined in. To further enhance the service, sunlight streamed through the great stained-glass west window to illuminate the interior bathing us in a multitude of colours. It was very impressive and for me was the best evensong ever.

16 St Mary's Church Shapwick

A year later at Harvest Home, I eagerly anticipated a repeat performance. Arriving in the church I was disappointed to find only a few more worshippers than usual and the evening was subdued compared with the previous year. Thinking it over later I recalled that because of bad weather the 1941 harvest had been relatively poor, many cereal crops were flattened in large patches and some rotted where they lay. It seemed that the irregular worshippers had stayed away that year out of resentment because better weather had not been sent and now had fewer misgivings about being absent. I have also thought since, that 1940 was a rather desperate year as far as the war was going for our nation with the Germans seeming all conquering. Perhaps those villagers who had attended in 1940 thought that they had best attend the service that year to keep God happy and themselves safe.

A little later, the produce donated to the church was auctioned off one evening at the village hall. Most villagers attended this event and bidding was often lively. Then a rare item was on offer; an orange! These had not been seen since the outbreak of war and a murmur of interest arose. I wanted it and when the bidding opened I quickly called out "Tuppence" which brought a roar of laughter from the audience much to my surprise. After all it was a bid but I only understood why it was laughed at when it eventually went for several pounds. The evening ended with a "bun fight" for the children. It had been eagerly anticipated because there were treats not usually available including lemonade. A few of the mothers served us as waitresses where we sat noisily at trestle tables in the gallery. One lady saw an empty platter and began replenishing it with buns. However, as she placed a bun another lady distracted her and she turned her head to chat. A boy quickly snatched the bun up. Then she placed another and again turned to talk and that bun was gone. This went on two or three more times. She then paused to regard the still empty dish, looked at our munching jaws and mischievous faces, to then burst into laughter as she finished loading the remaining buns.

Some of my mates decided that they would join the church choir. When I heard that they were accepted I wanted to be with them. When I told Mrs. Stevens that was my wish she said,

"If you join you must attend all services and there won't be any Sundays when you will be allowed to stay at home.".

This surprised me but thinking back, it was a golden opportunity for her to get me from under her feet for a while. Though this requirement gave me pause for thought because I was already attending Sunday school in the afternoons, I so wanted to be with my mates that I agreed. I applied to join and was accepted. In the vestry was a large cupboard containing a stock of surplices and cassocks used by successive choristers over the years. The older boys found one of each to fit me and I was soon clothed, white on black, doing my best to appear pious and holy. I did note that the black cassock I had was so old it had a greenish sheen to it. Although there were girls and a woman or two in the choir they went straight to their choir stalls upon arrival at church. We choirboys had the privilege of leading the vicar down the aisle at a slow dignified pace, smaller boys in front taller behind, all doing our best to look innocent. Females and males in their separate stalls faced each other across the choir aisle. One woman there had a particularly strong and shrill soprano voice that could be heard sailing high above all other voices. I think that she would have liked to be a diva in grand opera!

When the novelty as a choir member wore off, I realized what a mistake I had made. This was because I had to hear sermons twice on those days and attend Sunday school too. It was an overload of religion and the beginning of an aversion to religions that followed later in life. However, there were a few compensations because we had occasional small amounts of pocket money from the vicar and we got up to a little mischief whilst in the vestry before the vicar arrived and also when in the choir stalls during his sermon. The established choirboys had an initiation ritual for newcomers causing them to grab the newcomer and then thrust the vicar's vestry desk inkwell close under the victim's nostrils. Though the inkwell was dry it contained a stench that was nauseating. I was told that this had been caused some years earlier by one of the village boys having passed wee into it, which had dried leaving a horrible residue. What grubby little boys he and we were!

Very occasionally we were required to attend choir practice of an evening and that gave us an opportunity to run a bit wild around the village for a while after dark following dispersal. One escapade involved some small yew trees (more like tall shrubs) in the churchyard. They had grown several tall pole-like stems from a common base so we climbed high up these and rocked about as though on tall stilts. That would have been considered a sacrilegious crime if we had been caught but we never were. During one of these evening roamings we decided to play a prank on Happy Harry, proprietor of the village carpentry business. He was a self-appointed guardian of the villagers' morals and other behaviour and an unsmiling misery. The arrival of evacuees gave him an abundant opportunity to exercise his guardianship to the full. That evening we played the old London nuisance game of, "Knocking down Ginger". Why it was called that no one knew but it involved knocking on a house door and running away. Having hammered on Harry's front door knocker we rushed away to a safe distance and then relaxed and wandered about the lanes chatting and laughing together. We had forgotten the possible consequences of what we had done when, suddenly, Harry emerged out of the evening gloom scowling before us. There was a horrified shout of, "It's Happy Harry". We all rushed away to our respective homes as fast as we could. Once indoors I settled to one of my usual evening pastimes but it wasn't long until a knock was heard on the backdoor of Old Farm. Of course it was Harry come to complain about me whom he had recognised. Except for school attendance, I and others were confined indoors for two weeks for this misbehaviour. Of course that made us dislike Harry even more. I don't think that he was popular with the villagers either. I learnt later that he had a wayside chapel on the edge of Catcott, a village near to Shapwick, where it seems he was a Bible thumping, hellfire and brimstone kind of preacher who frightened the local children there with his self-righteous grumpiness.

Mrs. Seamer the vicar's wife, who played the church organ, was also the Sunday school teacher and a kind of choir mistress. After a year or so she asked me to pump the bellows of the organ during the services, an essential task if any sound was to be got from the instrument. I was pleased to be asked as it made a change from just singing. The bellows were pumped with air by a short wooden lever protruding from the side of the organ. There was a lead-weighted string next to the lever slot, also connected to the bellows, which indicated when being pumped how full they were by a series of score marks in the organ casing behind the string. The central heavily scored mark indicated the lower limit of air pressure in the bellows, below which the lead weight must not fall. I did this task successfully for several months and though enjoying it I began to experiment with the level of pressure I maintained. This went along alright and so I started to refine my technique by risking keeping the lead weight just above the central mark. Whilst so engaged, Mrs. Seamer hit a couple of bass notes on the organ expelling a rush of air from the bellows and the organ slurred its notes during a hymn. I received a startled look from the lady, who nodded her head vigorously to urge me to pump hard, which I did. Nothing was said when the service ended but the following Sunday I found I was demoted and a fellow chorister was now pumping instead.

Some boys discovered parts of church text that was thought rude or about sex. We devoured this information avidly. One text talked of virgins and wombs that we knew about, but during a Sunday school session, to cause discomfort, we asked of Mrs. Seamer with an air of innocence, what was the meaning of the virgin's womb? She was startled at this and with an air of embarrassment said that a virgin was a lady who wasn't married. She remained silent about wombs. She was a small, thin woman with a bird-like quickness and always dressed in black. She rode an upright bicycle to church or Sunday school when engaged upon her duties. If it was raining she cycled whilst holding over her head a large black umbrella. This was particularly impressive at a distance when seen over the perimeter hedge of Old Farm's orchard. As she sped down the road it was as though she was being transported by nothing else but the umbrella. She appeared to be a forerunner and older female version of Mary Poppins. Like so many clergymen's wives of those days she appeared active and alert in sharp contrast to her husband. He was rather large and overweight, quiet, somewhat ponderous and seemingly lost in thought most of the time.

During the last year or so of my stay in Shapwick we boys became aware of an invitation from a spinster who lived in top parish that she wished to conduct a Sunday school group in her home. She seemed to want to save our souls and, as she also offered light refreshments at the end of each session, we readily took up her offer. There was also another incentive in the form of a pretty and well-developed sixteen-year-old girl visitor, there for her summer holiday. For some weeks we attended to sing hymns in the spinster's front parlour as she and her friend beamed at us as we sang. We in turn beamed at the girl. On a weekday evening we boys took to lingering near the house in the hope of seeing this lovely creature when suddenly, a high attic window was thrown open and a note from the girl fluttered to the ground as the window closed. I can't remember the message it contained but it definitely showed an interest in us. We were delighted. A few days later we met the girl as she walked to the village shop. We engaged her in chat but she seemed strangely distant and cold towards us and after a few minutes of her reluctant responses we gave up and she walked away nose in the air. Thinking about this later we realised that from her attic window, she had a foreshortened view of us. Though we were wearing long trousers, she had gained the impression that we were taller and older than our twelve years. Moreover, from her high window she hadn't recognised that we were the same boys attending in the parlour. Our original ardour changed to frustrated dislike that was much increased when a week later we saw her walking out with one of the soldiers from the Shapwick House wartime temporary convalescent home.

At Kent Farm, outlying from the village, lived the Lockyer family including three sons who were in their late teens or early twenties. With their father, they worked on essential food production at this farm and so were not called for military service. They and their family were seldom seen in the village itself until the day that one of the brothers married. It was a lively affair with the bride in a white wedding gown (probably made from parachute silk like so many brides wore on their wedding day during the war). The village had been abuzz with this event and on the day a fairly large crowd assembled at the churchyard gate to watch including a large collection of boys, myself among them, having been told to expect a surprise. When the bride and groom emerged from the church and walked to gate they found it bound shut with wire and a toll to pass was demanded. The groom thrust his hand into a trouser pocket and withdrew a fistful of coins to throw over the gate and onto the road where boys frantically scrambled for them. The shower of coins comprised sixpences, shillings, florins and half-crowns and dependent on their values, brought varied levels of joy to those alert enough to quickly grab them. They were a small fortune to us. Then the gate was released and the couple was allowed to pass to climb into a black limousine waiting nearby with engine running.

There the other brothers were in close attendance with another man and when the bride and groom were settled these men grabbed the car's rear bumper and straining hard, lifted the back of the car off the road. The driver accelerated to move off but the car remained stationary as the men strained to hold it up. After a minute or two they dropped it and with a squeal of tyres off it raced trailing a collection of old shoes and noisy tin cans. These traditional rituals for a wedding were new to evacuees and we were delighted by them and looked forward to the next wedding but one never came before I had returned to Dagenham. I was told afterwards that the groom had taken coins from the wrong pocket as the other contained coppers he meant to throw but we didn't offer a refund.

12 THE MAJOR

In about ten acres of ground near the village centre stood a large and handsome Georgian house called "The Lawns". The house had the best-kept lawns and ornamental gardens in the village and there was also a kitchen garden and orchard. Here lived Major Royle and his brother Bertie, both bachelors. The Major seemed to be in his sixties and looked very fit being physically tall, slim and upright. His manner was polite if slightly gruff. He came about third in the social pecking order of the village. Game shooting was what he loved to do each season from September through the winter and engaged as much of his time in this as possible. He appeared to have permission to shoot over all lands within the parish, from Loxley woods above the village to a tract of the moors below. The range of game available to him included woodcock, pheasant, English and French partridge, pigeons, snipe, hares and rabbits. He must have also shot duck and similar waterfowl but I never witnessed that. Brother Bertie, his junior by a few years had no interest in shooting, appeared non-military and seemed not to do anything in particular. He was a more relaxed and easy-going person. The Major said that he had been a wonderful shot as a boy having brought down a blackbird in flight by a single slug from an air gun. That seemed to have revolted Bertie who never shot again. Both men were confirmed bachelors who employed two maids (Flossy and Margaret) to keep the house and cook for them. They also had a cleaner and a gardener. All of the servants were from Shapwick and lived out in their own cottages.

The Major kept the village people up to scratch by gently

browbeating them into things they might otherwise not have done such as attending church, buying National Saving Stamps, volunteering for Homeguard duties, etc. As he strode down the road he would bark, "Good day", at those he met. To the ladies he raised his checkered cap; to men he touched its peak with his walking stick in salute. Non churchgoers who saw him coming would discreetly withdraw indoors or slip away down a side lane until he had passed. It was curious that Bertie never attended church though The Major was there every Sunday Matins where, during psalms and hymns he unmusically barked out the words.

I first entered his palatial home to purchase a 15 shilling (75 new pence) National Savings certificate for which like many others, I had saved up some of my pocket money. Each Thursday evening he undertook this duty as a local organiser, being one of his contributions to the war effort. Those wishing to buy, entered the grounds by the main gate, walked up a gravel drive and entered the house via French windows. The Major sat waiting at a table in the corner of a large lounge, surrounded by sumptuous off-white furnishings. Underfoot similarly shaded, was a large deep pile Indian carpet with a restrained blue and pink pattern. For a room that was lived in, it was at the time the most splendid that I had ever entered. The business of savings certificates was transacted briskly and one was on one's way and out in a moment. Each early autumn, he invited a few evacuees to his orchard for a gift of "Beauty of Bath" apples, the earliest of the desserts to ripen in the season. At the appointed time, he met us at the orchard gate and we walked into the orchard. Walking beneath a tree, he paused to chat as he grasped a low branch in a seemingly relaxed pose. Then he unexpectedly shook the branch and grinned as we scrambled for the apples that fell around us. It was his little joke and we enjoyed it not least because we each left with an armful of fruit.

Each year a few of the older, stronger boys of the village, including evacuees, were invited by The Major to act as beaters and game bearers for the guns on one of his Saturday shooting forays. He preferred these boys because he was then confident that he would not have to carry game himself. Being small for my age in the early years of the war I did not get an invitation for this and as a result, felt envious of those that did. For a day of this activity, each boy received a picnic meal, a hot bath, a hot evening meal and two shillings and sixpence (twelve new pence, a handsome sum for a boy in those days). After a couple of years had passed and several evacuees had by then returned home, there was a shortage of large boys in the village. Despite the fact that I had hardly grown in that time, The Major adjusted his standards and I was now big enough to be offered, to me at least, the coveted invitation. Just before 9:30 a.m. on the chosen day, two other boys, Eric Day (from West Ham and billeted with The Major), Bob Grogan, and myself presented ourselves well clad with strong boots at The Major's house (back door this time). Prompt at 9:30a.m. The Major emerged tweed clad, including pork-pie hat, gaitered and booted, nap-sack containing sandwiches slung from a shoulder, double-barrelled shotgun under his arm, an ammunition belt and with "Tory" his faithful spaniel dog. Another elderly man who formerly may have been of the military who, similarly attired and equipped, always accompanied him with his dog which was a handsome black Labrador. This man did not live in the village but came by car from a distance. One of the maids gave us our packed picnic lunch and typically for these occasions, the party set off at a steady walk to Loxley woods. The men carried their guns "broken", that is, open at the breech for safety reasons to ensure no chance of them being accidentally fired. These hunts varied in the success of the amount of game killed but what follows is the essence of one of these excursions involving Eric, Bob and myself.

When in the wood, the party being few in number meant that it was impossible to drive game towards the guns so the whole group formed up in line abreast at about twenty-five yard intervals to beat through, a gun on each flank. By the time we emerged on the far side, we beaters carried a woodcock and a brace or so of pheasants. It was interesting to see the fine plumage of these handsome birds at close quarters. Next we came to a stubble field seemingly devoid of any wild life. Halfway across there was a sudden whirr of wings and after a quick blaze-away, we were then also carrying a brace and a half of partridge. Then we were into a field of fully-grown and hearted cabbages. As we walked the rows their turgid leaves squeaked as we brushed past them and they sometimes snapped. More gunfire and we then carried a brace of pigeons. As there had been heavy dew on the cabbages the night before, each boy had wet legs and socks when we emerged at the far side of this field. As our hands began to fill, The Major would stop to cut from a hedge two stout bearer sticks for each boy onto which each kill was suspended head down. Birds had a loop of twine slipped around their legs and rabbits had a slot cut in a hind leg between two bones. With the other leg passed through the slot, the rabbit's hind legs were fixed in a cross for the stick to be passed between them. Each time that a rabbit was bagged The Major took his penknife to slit the rabbit's paunch to expose its guts. With a sharp flick, he then caused the guts to be thrown from the animal into a hedge whilst its fore and hind legs were firmly gripped. Thus each stick loaded with a row of game was easily carried by hand at the point of balance. So it went on, the dogs retrieving birds and rabbits shot, including those birds downed but wounded that had run on. We walked ten or fifteen miles a day including going down to the moor for snipe. About mid-day we sat against a hedge to eat our sandwiches before setting off once more.

The Major remained alert all times during these hunts but his companion often walked along looking at the ground without paying attention to game rising before him. The sound of The Major's gun would bring him out of his reverie and though he fired he was often too late and some birds lived for another day. The Major was an excellent shot and usually got a kill with each barrel. Even in fairly dense woodland he usually got a sight and a kill. Some species of bird like pigeons and snipe seemed to take sharp left or right turn as evasive action in flight but he rarely missed them. He seldom needed both barrels attempting a kill and rarely missed then. Should he do so, he was highly embarrassed and very put out. Once in a turnip field as I stood next to him he missed a pigeon with both barrels. "Confound it", he barked. Red-faced and looking around his feet exclaimed, "I slipped on that beastly turnip! Caused me to miss!" Looking to where he stood it seemed to me that none of the turnips had moved and they were undamaged by being trodden on but I said nothing. As turnips are inclined to do they were standing there minding their own business. For the rest of the time in that field and until he had cleanly shot another bird we heard non-stop about that "Beastly turnip". Naturally, the more he went on about it the less we believed him. Later, after we had told our other friends about it, we adopted the phrase. Thereafter, should we slip in the school playground or miss our footing elsewhere no matter what the cause, we yelled, "Beastly turnip".

Nevertheless, The Major was a very good shot and little quarry escaped him. He occasionally got two birds with one shot but always made it clear that he only aimed for one. If a covey of partridges got up he aimed only at a bird on the edge of the flight. "It's bad form to shoot into the `brown`, he would say meaning where the covey was crowded. He went on to explain that if one did not observe that sporting axiom the proportion of birds wounded but not brought down would be high. This was cruel, as many would die a painful lingering death. He once shot a snipe but was convinced that he had also accidentally shot another bird. The rest of us had not seen any other bird involved but his sharp eyes had seen something. "Think it was a skylark", he said gruffly. Tory his spaniel, brought back the snipe and though unconvinced of anything else remained, was sent off again to search. After a few minutes he was back and indeed, carried a dead skylark The Major was rather upset at the sight but went on to say, "Used to be eaten you know; especially their tongues". It was an accidental hit but a great pity to us all. It was the first time I had seen a lark at close hand and was surprised at the length and delicacy of its spurs. The gun dogs were very good and seemingly tireless, retrieving all quarry shot. This included those that were injured. I never saw an instance of any injured creature not retrieved even though they had run a fair distance after being downed. When a wounded bird was in hand, breaking its neck quickly dispatched it. Both men competed to extol the virtues of their respective dogs and said, "What good mouths they had". Of course, this meant that the dogs had gently but firmly held game in their jaws without it suffering further damage.

At the end of a day shooting we arrived back tired, happy and hungry. Often we were also rather wet. The Major then sent us off to the maids in the kitchen where we took off our boots to be gently dried and cleaned. One maid went upstairs to run a bath for us and when ready we went off to the bathroom. She then took our clothes to the kitchen for drying by the huge range fired by anthracite. The bath was deep and at least two and a half yards long by about two feet wide. It did not have a conventional drain plug but an enamelled tube that did the same job but its open top acted as an overflow. Two huge taps fed the bath with hot and cold water and it easily accommodated we three boys for our communal bath. We were left to ourselves for about forty-five minutes when we were told to finish and come downstairs. When the bath was empty, Eric demonstrated a novel bath-time sport. Whilst naked, he slid on his back down the sloping end of the still wet bath meeting the taps end with the soles of his feet. Quickly flexing his legs he thrust back with enough force to almost slide back to the lip of the bath at the sloping end. He was an expert and repeated this trick several times in rapid succession but when Bob and I took our turns we each only ended up in a heap of flailing arms and legs.

After bathing, our clothes were returned warm and dry then we went to the kitchen for a hearty meal. Told that when we had eaten, The Major wished to see us, we later trooped into his study. There he sat by a fireside with his spaniel and his gun, both looking in good condition. He remarked on the day's events and gave a short lecture on how all such days should end. "First and foremost, look after the dog. Bathe it, dry it, comb and feed it. Next, clean, oil and check the gun. Then lock gun and ammunition away, each separate from the other. We don't want both falling into the wrong hands do we! These are the golden rules. Lastly, look after yourself. Never forget this boys", and giving each of us our two shillings and sixpence, ended with, "run along home now and goodnight".

We wondered where all of the day's game went that The Major and his friend shot on these excursions. Certainly they kept a share and the local landed gentry over whose property they had shot were each sent a prime selection as, no doubt, were special friends they may have had elsewhere. The rabbits and birds must have nicely supplemented their own and other wartime larders. But then, most if not all farmers and men in the village did likewise with rabbits and pigeons shot or trapped by them.

Because of this connection with the shooting parties and the fact that my close friend Eric Day was billeted with The Major, I was allowed to frequently visit The Major's property to play with Eric. Though we did not have the run of the house we had access to parts of the garden and most of the outhouses including the old stables and coach house. Several were no longer used and exploring them was interesting and fun. One summer holiday we found a web occupied by a large spider in the corner of a window within a dusty storeroom. It was the kind that people know as a cobweb. The spider lurked out of view within a silken tube and emerged only to kill any prey that fell into the web. We adopted it as a special pet and spent time now and then feeding it. This we did by catching flies with our hands as they basked on sunlit wooden doors and throwing them into the web. The spider quickly consumed the first few of these victims but it soon had a surfeit of food. Thereafter, all arriving insects were carefully wrapped by it in its silk for leaner times. By the time we grew tired of this project he had a very well stocked larder just like The Major. We had hoped to grow the spider to a giant of its type but big though it was originally and despite the generous food supply it never seemed to grow perceptibly larger. Again, just like The Major.

Eric had an air gun and when our funds could afford some ammunition (slug pellets), much of our time was spent in target practice. We used spent shot gun cartridge cases set up in rows or groups on a flight of steps or on walls. This was good fun too with a touch of competition and, I suppose, our imaginations led us believe that we were shooting German soldiers. When we had used up our ammunition, as it was scarce in wartime, we made a substitution. Several cabbage butterflies flitted about the gardens at "The Lawns" so we set about killing this pest. By loading the breech with a small amount of damp, gritty earth we could get closer to an insect than by any other way. By firing at close range, it was killed with a kind of grapeshot effect. Crazy though it now seems, we really enjoyed this.

The best game of all that we devised was with a ladder about twenty-five feet long. It hung horizontally on wall brackets on the rear wall of a lean-to outhouse that had clear headroom near the wall of about twenty feet. The front of this building was open except for timber roof supports and a strong fence about four feet six inches high. Though empty, this airy building was the sort that would have housed calves or heifers. By placing the ladder across the fence at the point of balance, we climbed onto it, one at each end, to create the best seesaw in the world. As the ground outside the fence sloped slightly down, it enabled the arc through which we travelled to be quite long. When riding, the ladder had a slow, ponderous movement. The one sitting within the building also had the unusual experience of floating roof-wards in a sedate manner, stopping just short of the rafters before descending. The one outside had an aerial view of its roof tiles.

This play went on intermittently for a few weeks but was ultimately the cause of our disgrace. The lean-to was separated from the house and gardens by a high wall set with a large door. One day whilst using the ladder The Major appeared at the door looking for Eric to run an errand for him. Seeing what we were doing he said in a firm but friendly voice,

"Don't use the ladder that way boys. Not good for it! Put it away and don't use it again." We quickly obeyed and that was that.

About two weeks later Eric and I had exhausted all pastimes available to us when Eric said,

"Let's use the ladder."

The idea having been raised we then discussed the rights and wrongs of it and, if we acted on it, what chance was there of being found out?

"Oh, it will be alright," said Eric, "The Major seldom comes through here. He'll not catch us."

Without further ado, out came the ladder and the pleasurable old game resumed. Within a few minutes the door opened and The Major walked through. The words he was about to utter died on his lips and he stood for a moment, a look of incredulity on his face. Then as his complexion turned purple he shouted in full parade ground manner,

"ERIC!"

There was a brief moment of silence as the ladder continued to carry me gently aloft. Both Eric and I knew that we were in serious trouble. We were already scrambling off of the ladder when The Major roared that we should do so. As soon as we had replaced it on the brackets we both got a furious dressing down. I was then told to depart and did so rapidly, white and trembling. As I went I heard The Major order Eric to report to his study in five minutes.

That signalled the end of my visits to The Major's property. Of course, he was right and we had let him down. It probably was the first time in thirty or forty years that he had knowingly been disobeyed. The final outcome was that my friend Eric found himself billeted elsewhere within the week. It was not long after that he returned to his parents in London and I lost a good friend.

13 DOGS

There was a motley collection of dogs in the village ranging from fairly large to very small and from the uselessly pampered to the highly trained and intelligent. Their colours and shapes were as varied as the individuals.

Sam was the dog at Old Farm and arrived one day as a puppy of about eight weeks old with his mother. He was a mongrel of a friendly, tolerant disposition with foxhound and spaniel in him. After about two weeks his mother returned to her owners and after a short time of moping for her, Sam settled down with us. He lived around the main living quarters of the farmhouse and garden each day. When the adults were about to go bed he was taken the short distance across the orchard to the barn where he slept. His purpose there was to raise the alarm in the event of intruders in the farmyard but there never were any. In theory his other main duty was as a cattle dog. Although he received some tuition in this, his efforts in rounding cows up to bring them to a destination always ended chaotically. He would set off purposely when ordered but he always got too close to the cows and individuals would chase him. He had several narrow escapes from thrusting horns. The end result at these times was that we had a herd of unsettled cows scattered widely. Because of this, Sam was retired from this responsibility and became more of a household pet. He was an almost constant companion to us boys around the farm. He also accompanied our friends and us on several of our adventures when we went roaming. Sam also had one or two adventures of his own.

As he grew from a puppy he became a handsome, black, brown and white dog. He had to make his way with others of his kind in the village but as a rule they did not mix much. It was an unwritten rule not to allow dogs to roam unattended. However, Mr. Langford the village baker had an old dog with strong territorial instincts that took a dislike to Sam. This was unfortunate as the bakery and its dwelling was almost opposite the main gate to the orchard of Old Farm. Whenever Sam accompanied us out of the orchard and up the main village road, he was obliged to run the gauntlet to escape this dog. This enemy always seemed to be patrolling his home usually from the top of a low stone wall capped with broad flags. Terrified, Sam slunk by almost pressed to the hedge opposite but with monotonous regularity he was spotted by the other dog that rushed at Sam with hackles up, snarling and snapping. Sam would flee in terror often getting a sharp nip to send him yelping on his way.

This state of affairs persisted for several weeks despite the efforts of we boys to drive the attacker off. The day eventually dawned when a showdown took place. Sam and we were passing the trouble spot and Sam was showing his usual nervousness but something distracted him momentarily. Suddenly the baker's dog was among us and had knocked Sam onto his back and stood over him snarling and snapping. Never before were things as serious for Sam as this. He was trapped so he could not run, neither could he rise. In desperation from his underdog position, he too snapped and snarled in retaliation. This startled the assailant and a moment's hesitation allowed Sam to gain his feet and then a fierce fight ensued. It did not last more than a few seconds with a crescendo of snarling and snapping but the first to break off was the baker's dog The tables were turned and he was put to flight, up onto the wall and around to the back of the bakery. Sam looked pleased with himself and our praise and patting must have added to his pleasure. Thereafter, Sam never cowered past the bakery but trotted by; head held high and tail waving. They never fought again because the baker's dog never dared to come down from his wall when Sam was passing but retreated, grumbling, into his garden.

Sam used to have about two baths each year and an occasional delousing when he started scratching too much. He hated both treatments and when suffering them, looked very forlorn. I am sure that after a bath he considered himself sissified and one time did something about it. As I have mentioned, most dogs were not allowed to roam the village because sheep and cattle worrying could result from individuals or packs of unrestrained dogs. Nevertheless, one day Sam and about five other dogs found themselves together without benefit of human company. No doubt following the usual preliminary enquiries and inspections of one and other, they were seen setting off as a rather ragtag and bobtail bunch along the lane towards Beerways Farm. Two or three hours later when I was by the back door of Old Farm, a somewhat jaunty Sam reappeared coming up the garden path blithely unaware that he was about to be in trouble. I happened to be just outside the back door at this time and went to meet him. As I got close I sensed a nauseating stench; it was coming from Sam and some slime on his coat. The only other creatures than he that appreciated the stench was a small cloud of flies that were his escort. I shouted rather sharply to him and his head drooped, his tail went between his rear legs and he lay down submissively. Fearing that he might attempt to enter the house I ran to the backdoor and called to Mr. Stevens. The urgency of my voice brought him quickly out and Sam tried to melt into the ground. Mr. Stevens had no hesitation in agreeing that the stink that surrounded the dog was particularly disgusting. With no further ado, he got the bathtub and filled it, took Sam by the collar and made him get into it. Sam was soon well soaped and then once more socially acceptable. It seemed that Sam and the other dogs had found an abandoned animal carcass that had been scavenged by foxes. The dogs had then rolled in the rotting flesh. In this way, Sam set a new record; three baths in one year!

Of all the dogs living in the village, the daftest was a bull terrier belonging to the Rev. Seamer, our vicar. There were other daft dogs but they were of the lap-dog type, pampered by one or two genteel, retired spinsters living in the community. These did not count as dogs in the eyes of we boys. The vicar's dog was typical of its bull terrier breed; white, thick set with pig-like pink rimmed eyes with a waddling trot. There was no harm in the dog as he was just an amiable idiot. He was usually in the company of the vicar's wife but occasionally escaped alone. We knew that the vicar had taught this dog to respond to one thing. A blast on a referee's whistle summoned the creature to a meal should it not be in sight within the vicarage grounds. One day this dog appeared in the orchard where we were playing football. The dog joined in for a while but was soon out of breath. As we stood looking at him and discussing his stupidity he stared up at us in a happy way. It was then that I remembered that there was a referee's whistle of sorts in the toy box indoors. Telling my friends that I had an idea, I went to get it. Upon my return the dog was lying on the ground panting and I explained to the others an experiment I had in mind. Standing at about ten yards from the dog and in the opposite direction to the vicarage I blew the whistle. The dog's head jerked up momentarily puzzled then scrambled up and rushed across the orchard, under the gate and up the street to its home. We had a good laugh at this and if we had owned a wooden bone, the dog would have had it as a reward. We tried the same wheeze once or twice later and it always worked. I guess that the animal was disappointed to find no food when arriving home.

Bill Durston, farmer and butcher, owned two small dogs. One was long and low like a black and tan dachshund and the other, her son, was similarly coloured but taller and broader He was the grumpiest dog in the village and all attempts to befriend him were met with a menacing growl. Both were regularly seen en route between the farm and the butcher's shop about a quarter of a mile up the hill. Mr. Durston rode his bicycle with his bitch running along free but with Grumpy on a lead, so the dogs were compelled to run as hard as their short legs would move. Every time they went up the hill Grumpy needed to urinate but the butcher never stopped for this to take place for the dog's comfort. Instead, the animal did his wee-wee on the trot and so created a noticeable splashy zigzag wet line on the road when it was dry for about fifteen or twenty yards. We boys felt sorry for the dog but we also got some amusement from the performance.

Major Royle owned one of the few working dogs in the village with a decent pedigree. As I have said The Major loved to go shooting small game about the village and his dog, a long-haired brown spaniel, accompanied him as a retriever on these forays. The Major had served in France in the Great War and had been wounded by a bullet in an arm. "Spun me around like a top", he once informed us. Continuing to serve after that war he was now long retired but in order that the world should be in no doubt with whom his political allegiances lay, he called this dog Tory. It seems to have reflected the high regard in which The Major held both party and dog but to call a dog a Tory, seemed a curious train of thought then and still does.

Perhaps the most impressive dog of all belonged to a labouring villager who in his spare time also managed his own small flock of sheep. The understanding between man and dog was a pleasure to see. At a quiet command the dog would round up the sheep, stop the flock, divert it or separate an individual from the rest all without fuss or aggression. He was an example to many other dogs, especially Sam.

14 HAYMAKING

To me a sweet part of summertime in Shapwick was haymaking, the first occasion for me being in June in the beautiful summer of 1940 (weather that is, but not the way of the world that year). The first cuts were in a narrow field next to one known as Croft, (pronounced "Criff") an ancient name I believe. Jack the pony pulled a hay cutter machine with Mr. Stevens holding reins as he controlled movements from a seat set over the wheels. As it was cut the grass was laid in swathe lines up and down the field. Its lower stalks and leaves were wet with dew and as it lay so a most sweet aroma arose. The village was soon bathed in this sweetness as other farms also made hay. Most of the village men, some women and many boys and a few girls helped with this. Whole families could be in these fields turning the swathes of hay to dry it. That year Granny Moxey was with us there in Croft for, as it transpired, the last time to do this work. When the swathes were dry they were drawn into lines by hand or horse-rake to be later heaped into haycocks set in ranks across fields in readiness for men with horse-drawn wagons to collect. Sometimes I did this horse raking with Jack the pony. The first time, after a ragged start, I got the gathered hay in mostly straight lines across the field each time that I pulled the release lever and that gave me the delusion that I was becoming a good farmhand but I did enjoy it.

Loading the wagons was done by the use of pitchforks. I could only reach up with my contributions when the wagon was less than three-quarters full before being diverted to another task in the field. When they had got the measure of me, the men put me on top of the wagonload with a man to spread the hay evenly in layers. As each pitchfork full of hay arrived from the ground it had to be quickly and evenly spread to balance and secure the wagonload. So loading continued through the ranks of haycocks with the horse halted with a "whoa" at intervals for loading. When it was time to move on, there was a warning shout of, "Hold vast (fast)" so that we on top could steady ourselves for the jerk as the horse pulled. A sense of readiness was needed to avoid falling, as sometimes the horse would anticipate the shout and move the wagon.

The hay from each load was then taken to be stacked in barns, rickyards or field corners. Building a neat stack was a skill and it gradually rose from a staddle of thick branches and brushwood laid in a rectangular layer a few feet high on the ground. This staddle or base helped to prevent dampness from the ground rising up into the hay. Mr. Stevens thatched his hayricks and straw mows himself, using either specially selected straw stalks, or reeds cut from the levels of Shapwick moors. He fixed the thatch in place with withy spars of hazel that held horizontal lines of twisted straw ropes or instead, long slender withy wands cut from the willows bordering the vegetable garden.

The great draught horses were in their element hauling their heavy loads of hay. They seemed to take pride in their massive strength, visible as rippling muscles under a shiny coat. One horse was an exception to this rule, as I will tell. We were working as a co-operative arrangement between Mr. Stevens and another farmer, Mr. Jennings. This meant that labour and equipment owned by each was pooled in an effort to get all of their hay crops dried, stacked as quickly as possible. Duke was a carthorse that had been borrowed for a few days from Manor Farm and with the mare, Pleasant, was working in a hayfield on Shapwick Hill. With one horse to each wagon both were being loaded. My Dad, who with Mum, was on a week's holiday, was with me at the time and enjoying helping with the work. As a friendly gesture to my dad and me, one of the farmhands said,

"Would the young-un like to ride on the horse?"

Seeing my face light up at this offer he immediately swung me up and onto Duke's back as he stood in the shafts.

Duke was a large Shire horse with a very wide belly. With me perched on his back, he stood placidly whilst the men continued to load. I had hardly sat there for a minute when another farmhand came to us and said,

"I know theck thar (that there) horse. He be a lazy, artful old bugger. I reckon you ought to get the young-un off him."

So, I was lifted down. Wondering what this meant, I had hardly got used to being back on the ground again when, with a thump and a jangle of harness, Duke fell down. This immediately caused a flurry of excitement among all present and I was told to sit on Dukes head as he lay. This was to prevent him struggling to rise whilst he was still harnessed to the shafts as there was a possibility that he would entangle and be injured. The men set about unhitching him as he lay. The man who had advised that I should not sit on the horse said

"What did I tell thee? That horse is the laziest old sod I ever did see. Look-see at his gurt (great) belly! What he needs is a bit less to eat and a bit more work. I tell thee young-un, thee had a narrow shave just then. E' only laid down cos of thee sitting on his back."

With Duke unhitched and me away from his head, the horse was encouraged to his feet and was briefly walked around to see that he was unharmed and then re-hitched to the shafts. Loading then recommenced but Duke's laziness was to be further confirmed a little later.

The field where we were was near the summit of Shapwick Hill. Its exit gate was up a fairly sharp incline leading onto the road. With a mighty heave, Pleasant pulled her full hay load towards the gate taking the lead and quickening her step as the wagon wheels met the incline. Duke and his load was to follow with Mr. Stevens who taking his bridle in hand, gave a command to go. Duke leaned into his task, the wheels did a half turn and the horse relaxed to a halt. Again the command but no movement from Duke, a further shout to move but nothing happened. Cutting a stick from the nearby hedge, Mr. Stevens handed it to another man and as the halter was grasped again, the stick was brought hard down on Duke's hindquarters. Apart from a flinch there was no reaction from the horse and the wagon remained still.

"It's no good treating him like that," said the man who knew the horse, "I keep telling thee, he's the laziest old sod I ever did meet. What thou hast to do is to think one better than 'e. What 'e be askin' fur is a helping hand with his work."

During all of this, Pleasant had been halted and was waiting several yards ahead.

Mr. Stevens, after a moment's consultation with the others said,

"We will soon see if his load is too heavy. Back the mare and her load to Duke so that it is about six feet ahead."

This was quickly done and Mr. Stevens, making rather a show of it, used the rope halter on Duke's head to thread it onto the rear of the forward wagon in pretence to tie it. With a man to each horse's bridle and with simultaneous commands to move, the mare once more leaned into her task. As her wagon rolled, so Duke also took the strain of his load and both wagons rolled up the incline and onto the road. The remarks of the man who knew the horse were reconfirmed and the rest of the men just shook their heads saying that they had not seen the like before. One further little incident that happened was that as the wagons moved, so the halter rope soon fell loose from the leading wagon and hung from Duke's head. For all his artfulness Duke had gained no help at all and I think that if he had been a little brighter and human he would have spent his life dodging work and living off the dole.

During haymaking our midday meals comprised of bread and cheese if we were at a distance from the farmhouse. Sometimes a picnic was brought to us and placed on a tablecloth spread on the ground. These were heartier meals and, as with the bread and cheese, were washed down with cider. We boys were also allowed a small amount from the gallon stone jar but it was not much to our liking as its taste was sharp. As evenings stayed light till 11 p.m. because of double British Summer Time, loading and stacking the hay continued late with the last load coming into the rickyard after 10 p.m. Though boys were allowed to stay up late if there was no school the following day we usually left for bed before 10 p.m. When the final load had been stacked and daylight failed, supper was brought to the hot and tired men who sat on spilt hay at the base of the rick for the meal. Though drinking was not overdone during the day, during these suppers the gallon jar was passed around and conversation livened with yarns and comments being murmured among the men. This quiet conversation then gave way to anecdotes about times long past or recent and the various characters in the community they had known. Then some jokes and mildly ribald remarks as the generous supply of cider took effect.

17 Dad

My dad thoroughly enjoyed his holiday that coincided with the end of the season's haymaking and working with the team. He told me that after the final supper when all of the hay was in and the hayrick completed, it was necessary for a large canvas sheet to be spread over its top to provide protection from rain. Someone from the group was needed to climb a tall ladder with the heavy sheet on his back. Dad said that the biggest man in the group was jokingly challenged to get it there. He started in his attempt but only got partway up the ladder before swaying, almost losing his balance and letting drop the sheet to a chorus of friendly chiding from the others. All of the big men took their turns but it was a difficult task and strong though they were, they could not do it and each failure was met with more cheerful banter. These failures may have been partly due to the intake of cider. Then it was the turn of Mr. Stevens.

Though broad shouldered and sturdy he was only a few inches over five feet tall. Shouldering the burden he took to the ladder and to the surprise of all present, got it to the top. Others then came up to spread and secure it and so the hay was safe should rain have come before thatching. My dad was very impressed by the strength and ability of Mr. Stevens that night.

On still and hot summer evenings as I lay in bed, I listened to sounds of the last wagon creaking into the farmyard. A little later the released horses were heard cropping the orchard grass as the last light faded and sleep overtook me. This haymaking was hard work for the men as they had been at work since 6 a.m. each day for milking and then at haymaking all day before more milking at around 6 p.m. and afterwards, back to the hayfield in the evening.

The next morning after the hayrick was completed a long pole was slipped under the canvas at its ridge and supported by other poles, lifted clear to make a tent-like shape. The gap created allowed ventilation of the stack to reduce the risk of it catching fire as a result of spontaneous combustion because new hay heated significantly. I recall climbing into the "tent" and it was as though entering a sauna, hot, humid and stuffy. Though I never saw it happen I was told that when a rick seriously over heated it had to be dismantled, dried further and rebuilt usually because the hay was too green or rain damp. So when building a stack, good judgment of the hay condition was vital.

As I have mentioned above, Mr. Stevens and another farmer, Mr. Jennings, had a co-operative arrangement at haymaking where they combined their resources to speed the work. It seemed to operate on the basis of mutual trust and it worked well. Tractors were not available to either of these two farmers so horses were the haulage power source. However, one year, Mr. Jennings acquired a two and a half litre Ford car that served partly as a tractor. This powerful motor was stripped down to its bare essentials of chassis, wheels, engine, front seats and a modicum of bodywork such as mudguards. The rear of the chassis was boarded over and so was used to carry quickly here and there, small loads, workers and we boys as necessary. This vehicle came into its own for haymaking for not only did it get the team of workers quickly to distant fields but also it had another great advantage. A strong metal frame was fixed onto the front of the car to receive some attachments including a sweep. This comprised of about eight square wooden poles, seven feet six inches long and set one foot apart, all pointing forward. These were tapered and metal shod at their pointed leading ends that curved slightly up like skis. The whole formed a comb-like framework close to ground surface and when driven into swathes of dry hay, collected it in a front loaded heap. This was then rushed to the hayrick where it was left for stacking and the car and sweep backed off to then repeat the process. It did away with raking by hand or horse rakes, haycocks, horses and wagons. It was great fun to ride on the boards on the back of this car by holding tight. The road surface could be seen rushing by between and below the boards causing our gripping hands to become even tighter as we bowled along the lanes. It was what is now known as a "white knuckle ride".

15 SMOKING

To many young boys in the 1940's, one of the hallmarks of being a real man was a smoking habit. Virtually every man worth his salt smoked and so did all of the tough-guy heroes that we saw on rare visits to a film show at the Bridgwater Odeon cinema. Mr. Stevens occasionally smoked a sweet smelling Gold Flake cigarette.

It was a youth nicknamed Ryder who really started us smoking when my friends and I were about twelve years old. He was not from Shapwick and had a job making deliveries by bicycle to various local villages. He was in his late teens, heavily and awkwardly built and adept at a smart line of small talk. In a teasing kind of way he delivered his thoughts to us, liberally laced with swearwords. He also had poor eyesight and peered myopically through spectacle lenses about as thick as bottle bases. It was probable that his weak eyes excused him from call-up for wartime military service. We supposed that Ryder got his name because he only appeared among us riding his bike. Remarking this to one of the older village boys we were told bicycles had nothing to do with it. It seemed to be a well-known fact that if two pairs of legs were seen protruding from any haystack next to Ryder's delivery route, it was a near certainty that the hairiest ones were his. The informant then added as an afterthought, that having seen some of the ladies that Ryder was familiar with, the hairiest pair of legs were not necessarily his, though that did not mean that he was absent at the time. Having the kind of job he had must have assisted him in his hobby of closely inspecting hayricks.

Another of Ryder's vices was, of course, smoking. Having met him by chance one sunny June day outside the village shop we found him in a very good mood. (He was probably pleased about all of the new hayricks being built for his benefit at that time of year). So he generously gave my friend Bob Grogan and I, a whole cigarette to share. Hiding behind a hedge we lit up for our first ever smoke. Our first puffs were tentative and though the taste was peculiar and unpleasant we both declared it good. Bob said that we should be taking it down with a deep breath as was proper for men. We attempted this and were immediately thrown into paroxysms of coughing and spluttering. Still we persisted and finished our halves to the last half inch. "How do you feel?" I asked Bob. "Fine he replied, despite his streaming eyes. "So do I", I lied, for not only were my eyes streaming I felt decidedly dizzy too.

On another afternoon, Sid Witherington, (who had later replaced Frank as my companion evacuee at Old Farm) and I each acquired a cigarette. We took them to a copse next to the old Roman road at the top of Shapwick Hill. Seated on a log we settled to a quiet smoke. When about halfway through mine I again experienced dizziness but as before, attempted an air of nonchalance. Glancing at Sid, I knew instantly that he was in a much worse state than I was. His head drooped to his knees and his complexion had taken on a greenish pallor. To assist his recovery, I attempted a few humorous remarks that immediately caused him to throw up the whole of his mid-day meal. I don't know what this did for Sid but it certainly frightened me. I resolved there and then never to smoke again if he would not die on the spot. About half-an-hour later he recovered and my resolution was forgotten.

Smoking among the boys of about eleven years and more became the thing to do, stupid though it was. The trouble was that for us, cigarettes were hard to come by as they were expensive and should we attempt purchases at the village shop suspicions would be aroused. Substitutes were sought and we experimented widely, finding dead leaves of oak or beech being acceptable tobacco alternatives. The next problem was with cigarette papers as these too were scarce and difficult to roll anyway. School exercise book paper, newspaper and even brown paper were all tried. Though each in turn was declared alright and of pleasant taste the truth was that none were, particularly brown paper. Attention was then turned to pipe smoking and we strained our brains to find a solution to pipe making from the woods and hedgerows. The first attempt was to cut off the tops of green acorns and hollow them out to form a pipe bowl. The next difficulty was finding a pipe stem and this was tricky. The best answer was the use of uncrushed wheat straws and by pushing them into a hole bored near the base of the acorn shell, a fair representation of a churchwarden pipe was fashioned. The problems were that being small, the bowl had to be refilled frequently, it tended to be insecure in its attachment to the straw stem and it or the bowl tended to quickly dry out to catch fire after a smoke or two.

Thus the search for the schoolboy's ideal smoker's pipe continued till eventually, one of our group hit on the idea of using stems from Japanese Knotweed. This overcame most of our problems. This plant was growing in a dense clump in the woods next to the drive within the grounds of Shapwick House where we often trespassed. The red and green mottled stems that reached a height of up to six feet are hollow with strong internodes. At its base a stem is up to an inch and a half diameter and the uppermost stems long and slender. Using living stems, we cut below a lower internode and then two inches above it to fashion the bowl. By the use of a slender stem from the top of the plant we fixed it into the bowl as with the acorn type. Thus, we had a device that looked distinctly like an American corncob pipe. They were popular with we boys, easily made, easily disposed of if adults were near and easily dismantled for carrying secretly. As the stems were green they resisted catching fire until they dried out after five or six smokes. Then they would flare with a crackling sound. As we sat around puffing at these we must have looked a bit like little old men sitting around a campfire telling yarns. I don't suppose any of us really enjoyed them but we pretended that we did and it was a part of our growing up.

One of the boys had a young dog that often came with us on our roaming. We made a pipe for him and he would clench it between his teeth. He too looked as though he enjoyed a smoke but of course, he never had anything in it nor did we light it. We boys never revealed that we smoked these pipes but when we walked the lanes with this dog and his pipe, it gave some of the village adults amusement as well as ourselves.

Perhaps the worst thing that was smoked was Elder pith. Some lads discovered that thick, dead stems from these bushes each contained a long, cylindrical pith about one inch thick. By cutting it into short lengths and pushing a nail through to make a tube, smoke could be drawn through when the end was lit. They were horrible to taste and smouldered quickly away of their own accord. As they grew shorter so the smoke tasted hotter and hotter until tonsils almost scorched. I only tried it once and the other lads soon dropped the idea. After that our smoking was mostly confined to an occasional cigarette scrounged from Ryder.

16 SHOPS

An ever-present problem for people during the war was the reduction in the supply of food, clothing and other commodities through rationing or scarcity. Living in the countryside meant that there were, relatively speaking, plentiful supplies of some things like eggs, vegetables, fruit in season and milk. However, foodstuffs that had undergone some process or other, e.g. tinned goods, and cheese were often unavailable, though farm workers got a double cheese ration. Exotic fruits such as oranges were rarely seen and bananas, never. Shapwick villagers also had to cope with the fact that that there were few retail outlets available. Apart from the Albion pub (a mile away at Pedwell), the village had only a small family butcher, a baker, post office and a general store. Because of rationing, the trade of the village butchers shop, run by the Durston family, had been reduced to a vestige of what it once had been. Much of its trade must have also suffered from the advent of butcher's rounds-men as practiced by the Cousen's butchery at Ashcott for whom Mr. Stevens worked. For our village butcher at least, perhaps it was just as well that his trade was run as an adjunct to his farm. Mr. Langford's village bakery ran a steady trade through its delivery van service to the district. Everyone got a fair share of baked items provided a strict control was kept on the sale of jam-tarts and sugar-puffs to us village children. They were a delicious substitute for scarce sweets and we once caused the bakery to run out of these and that upset the regular customers.

On some days during a school summer holiday Bob Grogan and I had a wonderful time at this bakery as the assistant baker allowed us to watch him prepare the dough and other items. He apportioned dough into the correct weight for each loaf and then kneaded them in pairs one in each hand into flattened spheres. As our interest grew so we were given a chance to do the same but it was easier seen than done. By way of compensation for our poor efforts we were each given a remnant of dough that we rolled into two strips and then plaited them together. With the large oven already hot and with the use of a long wooden paddle, the loaves and our plaits were slipped in and left to bake. There were variations on the loaf types; some in tins and others of the cottage sort with a small round loaf perched atop of a larger one beneath. Some loaves were given several angled cuts with a sharp knife to create a simple pattern before baking. When baked, our plaits were delicious, as were the loaves. That bread was how it should be made. We also saw how by rolling flat a large slab of raw pastry and then folding and rolling it several times more, made puff pastry when baked. The frequent folding caused the pastry to become layered. We thoroughly enjoyed these bake-house visits not least for the wonderful smell of baked bread within.

 The bailiff's wife ran the post office from a ground floor room that was part of the main dwelling at Church farm. It seemed that she combined this work with her domestic responsibilities. If someone entered her office, it was often the case that she was absent but would quickly appear from the main house in response to a bell. The general store was in its way more of a social centre and with the exception of the bakery, was a much more interesting place than the other shops. It sold everything from groceries, cigarettes, nails and hardware, to dry goods, clothes, shoes, etc. It had its own vaguely pleasant smell being a mixture of polish, tea, flour, oil, soap and dust. Its stock of clothes was small and seemed ten years behind the fashions of 1939. Ladies floral prints on offer all looked large and shapeless. Hanging from the ceiling in a corner of the store, they seemed to have been there years. The store was run in the manner of the times. A customer or two needing a number of items sat on bentwood chairs next to the counter whilst the shopkeeper and her teenage daughter, "Bunty", ran to and fro behind the counter bringing each item separately when asked. Sometimes we children were served our sweet ration quickly but at others we waited whilst a large order was served to one of the village women. Even then it could be interesting, as the shop was a centre for the dissemination of gossip. One could catch snippets of recent scandal, punctuated by sighs, tutt-tutts and exclamations as news was imparted by the one and received by the other. The juicier morsels of the exchanges were usually denied us, either by hushed words passed at close range with eyes resting on our pricked ears, we being just out of range. Otherwise silence reigned and we were served out of turn with conversation resuming on our departure.

Though the shop owner did her best, the range of goods had its limitations and should a national distribution difficulty arise the shop then ran out of some goods entirely. It was a real crisis for us young people if it happened to be the sweet ration. The shortage of sweets caused some among us to find substitutes. One of these was Oxo cubes that a few boys sucked gaining a very brown tongue in the process. Having tasted a fragment I found the strong salty flavour repulsive and had no wish to repeat the experiment. Some boys decided to try an unconventional form of chewing gum. Finding some blocks of bitumen at a roadwork site, they chipped of some clean flakes popped them in their mouths to chew. Their body heat was enough to render it malleable but not sticky. They pretended that it was good but when I tried some it was tasteless and that was the end of that experiment for me.

Shopping was supplemented by visits to Street, Glastonbury or preferably Bridgwater where the choice of shops and goods was much greater. These trips had the disadvantage of a journey by a single-decker bus on a service that ran about every two hours but children enjoyed the ride except for Norman who suffered from travel sickness. There were two services, the National Bus running along the top road about one mile away or the Bristol Blue Bus passing through the village. Sometimes, and especially regarding the Bristol Blue, the required bus arrived packed to the doors to pass by the would-be passengers non-stop. The long wait for the next bus usually caused the trip to be abandoned for another day. What few cars there were had mostly been laid up for the war's duration. Those that weren't, were for essential activities and they were strictly limited in their use by petrol rationing coupons.

18 Mum and Dad on a visit to Glastonbury Abbey

There was another unofficial source of scarce food that was known to only a few. It was the secret slaughter of a few pigs and bullocks. Because of wartime rationing this was forbidden by law and so carried risks of prosecutions. One Saturday morning I walked into a secluded part of the orchard to see Mr. Stevens busily shaving the carcass of a recently slaughtered pig. When finished he slit its belly and removed its guts for burial but before doing so separated the intestines. At this, a nauseating stink arose causing me to retreat to a distance of about fifteen yards to save myself from vomiting. Mr. Stevens carried on unconcernedly for as a skilled butcher, he was used to this work and was unaffected. Having cleaned the abdominal cavity he rinsed the intestines in clean water. He then took up a stick stripped of its bark, knotted an intestine over one end and proceeded to turn it sleeve-like inside out over the stick in readiness for use as sausage skins after washing. Later the pig was cut into joints, etc, and shared between its owner and others in the know. Similarly on another day in one of the farm's barns, I found a gutted bullock still with its hide, suspended by its hind legs. Though I did not witness its butchering I am sure it followed the same kind of distribution as the pig. I was a bit worried by an incident concerning the bullock. On the day following my discovery, I saw Mr. Stevens chatting to the local policeman over the farmyard gate whilst the carcass was still hanging hidden a few yards away. I was relieved that there were no following repercussions after the "Bobby" had left. Years later it crossed my mind that the "Bobby" was in on the conspiracy for though he occasionally was seen around on his old fashioned upright bike, he was never in the back lane next to the farmyard.

Mr. Stevens was a kind, easy-going man who was not of a nature to do anyone harm though he must have seen a great deal of blood and death in his work as a butcher. Despite this as he once told my Dad, he was not inured to the sight of human bloodshed. He went on to say that when he was a young man he joined a search party organised to look for two men missing from their homes in a local village. These men were rivals for the affections of a local girl. After ranging through fields and woodland for many hours, one man in his search group came across the bodies of the missing men. One had killed the other with a shotgun blast and then turned the gun on himself. Upon hearing this news, Mr. Stevens collapsed in a dead faint.

17 BUTCHER DURSTON

One autumn day, three of my mates and I helped ourselves to some apples from the orchard at Old Farm having had permission for this at any time. As we munched them, we went for a walk along Back Lane until we came to a five-barred gate set a few yards back from the lane. This led to The Major's orchard and we clambered onto it like birds at roost to continue eating. As we sat there, who should come up the lane but Butcher Durston riding in his smart pony-drawn trap. With barely a glance in his direction we continued to chat amongst ourselves as we chewed away. A great roar suddenly split the air and we saw that it came from the butcher and, having fixed our attention on him, we were horrified to see that he was heading in our direction fast. Not only that, his usual florid complexion had turned purple. Even worse he brandished a whip taken from a socket on the trap. Though he was rather stout he showed a turn of speed that day we would not have guessed he possessed. We knew immediately that he thought that we had stolen apples from The Major's orchard. None of us thought it prudent to remain on our perch to reason with him, knowing his reputation for a quick and violent temper. In a trice we had scattered with him lashing his whip at us this way and that but without making contact. We were all terrified and I heard myself whimpering with fright as I slipped past the furious man. But to where could I escape? The lane was narrow and confined by hedges except for a pond that broke its continuity. The pond's margins were overhung by the hedge providing a partial screen opposite to where all of the action was taking place. The pond served as a water source for cattle in a field I knew well as belonging to Old Farm.

Fearful that I would feel the lash at any moment, glancing back, I jumped onto the pond's muddy margins. I intended to work my way along its edge or if hotly pursued, through the water. Partially screened, I could see that the butcher was concentrating his chase on Hoppy Hopkins the biggest boy among us. Hoppy was showing remarkable agility in avoiding the lash and as he fled he was pursued by shouts of, "You young bugger! I've been after thee fur some time and now I have 'e!" But with a feint, Hoppy changed direction and dodged past him and ran off down the lane as fast as his legs could carry him. It was over as quickly as it had begun. Swearing and threatening us, our would-be assailant climbed back into his trap and with a flick of the whip to the pony, was off up the lane.

Crouching and trembling by the pond I found that mud had welled up over my boots almost to the laces but before emerging onto the lane I made sure that the enraged man had gone. My companions also emerged from their hiding places except for Hoppy who had gone home. It was remarkable that by co-incidence, he was billeted with The Major who of course owned the orchard! We others thought that Hoppy's example was one we should follow so we too trotted off to our homes. The next day we all met again and Hoppy said that he had not been struck but it was a close thing. Considering the butcher's rage we had all got off lightly but thinking back, perhaps he intended to give us a fright and not to actually strike us. He succeeded in giving us a nasty shock but we felt that we were victims of an injustice as he had assumed we had been "scrumping" (the term given to apple stealing). We agreed that he had only really been after Hoppy and had perhaps, used the incident as an excuse to settle some old score or resentment. When Hoppy was asked if he knew why this should be, he said he did not know but the rest of us thought he did; but wasn't saying. We also supposed that Butcher Durston had bought the apple crop for why would he chase us on behalf of The Major? Afterwards we avoided the butcher for a time and thereafter kept a wary eye on him should our paths cross.

18 CUCKOO

It was generally acknowledged each year that spring had really arrived when the first cuckoo was heard. In my second springtime in Somerset I eagerly told Mr. Stevens that I had heard one call. In reply he smilingly said,

"Oh, well, we will see Cuckoo Wainwright about the village any day now.".

As I looked mystified he explained that this man who lived with his daughter in a cottage in Church Road did not like winter weather. For many years he had taken to his bed at the end of September to avoid the cold. He did not come downstairs until the first cuckoo was heard the following spring. It then occurred to me that although I had seen Mr. Wainwright now and then in the past as a passing acquaintance, I had not seen him for a long time. About three days after I had heard the cuckoo call, sure enough, there he was out for a walk in the village.

19 MONTY TRATT

Monty Tratt was a farmer who served the village with a milk round from his farm on the edge of Shapwick Moor. The milk was brought door-to-door in a large old-fashioned churn drawn on a float by perhaps the slowest horse in the village. Most villagers were served their daily milk requirements in this way. As the horse with head drooping waited by a cottage gate, milk was poured by Monty from a tap near the base of the churn into a small lidded pail that he carried to dispense measured pints or halves by dippers. Using these measures, the correct amounts were poured into jugs provided by his customers. The horse could afford to be slow because Monty had to walk about three times as far as the horse as he had to negotiate footpaths and entries too narrow for the float. Moreover, Monty was not very quick on his feet. Having done the round for several years, the horse knew as well as the man where to stop, when to wait, for how long and when to move on. It would also anticipate the next call or go to meet Monty when he was due to appear several houses along a lane having served at several backdoors in a row. Village wags said that Monty had once sent the horse and float out alone on the round but abandoned the experiment because he was upset as the horse did it quicker and kept the books neater.

The fastest vehicles in the village were six-wheeled lorries engaged on the construction of wartime secret radio and aircraft detection installations near the top of Shapwick Hill. When un-laden, these heavy open-backed lorries were frequently driven down the hill and through the village at speeds in the region of fifty to sixty m.p.h. This practice was very dangerous but apart from some mutterings about it by adults, nothing more was said because, after all, it was essential war work that they were engaged on. Three essential elements were in position one fateful day. Mrs. Argent had not yet gone into her front garden for a gossip with passersby; Monty and horse were on the round; and a lorry was speeding down the hill. As usual and without being told, the horse plodded along Church Road adjacent to the churchyard wall. With the sound of the lorry approaching, Monty was behind the float heading for the corner cottage gate of Mrs. Argent. Slowly with head drooping as usual, the animal and float began to emerge towards the centre of the crossroads. The speeding lorry was now very close. With the shriek of tyres, the driver applied his brakes as horse and float hove into view. Too late! Swerving to avoid carnage and a lot of spilt milk, the lorry careered into Mrs. Argent's substantial front garden wall. In a shambles of stones, mortar and bits of lorry, the vehicle came to rest half in and half out of the garden and precisely over the spot where Mrs. Argent was in the habit of standing to gossip. After their initial fright, Monty and his horse carried on as before.

Thereafter, lorries from the construction site passed through the village at reasonable speeds and Mrs. Argent had a lucky escape. After the wall was repaired, there she was at her usual station and chatting, as was her custom.

Undeterred by the crash, her philosophy was obviously based on the theory that lightning (and lorries?) don't strike twice in the same place.

20 MISS VILE-STRANGWAYS

When young, Mrs. Stevens served this lady as a lady's maid and whilst going about her work, was frequently subject to lectures on the women's suffrage movement at the time. Mrs. Stevens told me that this talk was beyond her understanding, as it was never mentioned at the village school and newspapers were not available to her. This gentlewoman was the last in the line of an ancient family whose ancestry was recorded on various memorials to their dead set up in the cloisters of Wells Cathedral within whose See the village lay. They were lords of the manor of Shapwick who owned and lived in a superb mediaeval mansion set in well-kept grounds slightly below the village centre. Before the Reformation, these buildings were owned by and occasionally lived in by the abbot of Glastonbury Abbey. During my time in the village, Miss Vile-Strangways was over ninety years of age, frail, tiny, very pale, with wisps of white hair. If seen about the village she was always clothed entirely in black.

Like her ancestors, she lived in the mansion accompanied by a lady companion and a small retinue of servants. She was seldom seen out of doors except to arrive at church for matins each Sunday when well enough to attend, always supported by her companion. Unlike the villagers who entered the church through a porch on its south side, this lady and her companion entered and left by a private door just above the nave and into the sanctuary close to the altar and, presumably, nearer to God.

19 Me looking smug outside Wells Cathedral

It seemed that they were too proud and grand to be in touch or even near the common people. When I was in the choir I was able to get a closer look at the couple as they joined in the service. How they could follow the sermon I cannot say because the pulpit was several yards away and the vicar preached his sermons to the congregation facing away from these ladies. Perhaps they had no need of his words or found the quiet interlude restful. Still, they got full benefit from the blessing from the altar at the conclusion of the service. Was the amazing family name corrupted from the French, "Ville", perhaps? With an "e" after the "g" in Strangways it would have been even more remarkable.

Despite the austerity of the times Christmas remained a joyous occasion, its advent creating a particular excitement in the village setting. Carols were practiced at school, Sunday school and church. This was put to profitable use on the Saturday morning before Christmas Day when children were permitted to call house-to-house in the parish to sing carols. A group of about ten boys gathered for this (girls were never with us and I don't know why). We ranged far and wide getting a few coppers here and there and the occasional silver coin, a sixpence but never more than a shilling between us. One of the most awe-inspiring calls was to Miss Vile-Strangways then over ninety years of age at her ancient Manor House standing in its setting of lawns, shrubberies, ancient outbuildings and trees many of which were decrepit. We mounted the front steps of this beautiful place to tug on a bell-pull at the main door. A maid, who opened it, told us to wait and then shut the door. She reappeared a few minutes later, invited us in and ushered us along a passage and up a short flight of wooden stairs through a panelled area and into a large room. At its end sitting lopsidedly in a large armchair on a dais was the lady of the manor seeming even smaller and frailer than ever. The black of her clothes heightened the near transparent pallor of her face and her white wispy hair. Her thin face smiled wanly in greeting. Beside her sat her middle-aged companion, also in black, who bid us welcome. Keeping a sharp eye on us she said we could begin. Off we went with the choicest of our repertoire, singing at our very best. After about three carols the companion said how much Miss Vile-Strangways had enjoyed our singing. The old lady smiled again fluttering a hand in agreement. The companion then stepped from the dais and gave each of us an apple, a pear and a penny; or so I thought. We all said thank you to the ladies and were shown out by the maid. Standing out in the road we discussed our gifts and Ron Buttleman the oldest among us at thirteen, showed us a ha'penny and said, "That's all I got". We realised then that he had been penalised because his voice had recently broken and he had been hitting a few notes off key intermixed with gruffness and squeaks. We thought that he couldn't help his voice and that an apple, a pear and a ha'penny from a wealthy lady was mean. I have since wondered whether Ron's display of emerging masculinity was deemed inappropriate before a maiden lady or whether he merely spoilt the effect of our angelic (?) voices.

20 Shapwick Manor House

21 POULTRY

Any farm is very likely to have a flock of chickens but when I arrived at Old Farm there were only about twelve old Rhode Island Red hens. They were a novelty to Frank and me and in our ignorance we occasionally chased them about the orchard enjoying their cackling panic. We were asked not to do that because we had stressed them and they were going off their egg production as a result. They lived free range and were fed wheat twice per day, a job we liked as we scattered the seed on the ground. When they saw us doing this they came cackling from all corners as fast as legs and wings could bring them. At night they roosted on the side of an empty wagon in an open sided cart shed, flying up at dusk to be relatively safe from foxes. Like most domestic chickens, they had almost lost the ability to fly so this roost was at their limit. It was decided to get a cockerel of the same breed so chicks could be raised. When he arrived we saw he was a beautiful red with plenty of gold, his elaborate tail feathers shot through with iridescent shades of blue and green. Bright red wattles and large comb topped off his handsome appearance and he was very conceited. On his first day with us he strutted about his harem letting them know who was boss by frequently crowing and mounting each of the flock in turn. The hens seemed very pleased with him. As this first day ended, one by one the hens flew up to roost. The cockerel seeing that this was the thing to do strutted over, took flight and crashed into the wagon's side ending a heap on the ground. Regaining his feet he muttered a few clucks and did a bit more strutting and tried again but with the same result. Again and again he tried but without luck. Later in the gloom he was seen alone and dejected, perched in a lowly position on a wagon shaft.

This performance went on every evening, as he became desperate to join the hens, but still without success and his ego suffered. He obviously had been kept in a coop that required only low roosting as he was so physically unfit to reach the new perch. It took over a week for him to become fit enough. Once he was, he sat with the hens in a row with him centre and the hens in a pecking order of seniority on each side. After his showing off in so many other ways he had finally achieved the seemingly impossible. There must be a moral here somewhere. We could not help teasing him a bit when he crowed. After a pause we crowed back in a fair imitation and he always became very angry. This caused him to grab one or other of his wattles and give it a chewing. It must have hurt but I suppose he was firing himself up for a fight. We stopped teasing when we realised that he had chewed so much that his wattles were covered in scabs.

Of all of these birds none was quite so nice as Jenny. This old hen had over the years somehow managed to avoid the pot and even the Christmas poultry orders. She had become very tame, took food from hands and allowed herself to be stroked. Her enduring delight was tearing dried cowpats apart to find grubs spending their formative period there. The trouble to her was that the pats became very hard baked in the sun so she waited next to one if someone was near. She clucked by way of asking for help and by using a stick, the baked surface was lifted like a lid when she then made short work of the grubs revealed. Occasionally, we had a surprise when a hen appeared with a group of chicks that she had incubated secretly in a hidden nest somewhere within the rickyard.

As the years went by these chickens had many more companions and the company of other flocks of poultry. For someone of a nervous disposition, the most frightening of these were geese. They would come at anyone who passed near them, holding their necks out at full stretch and hissing in a threatening way. It was all show though, for if the person threatened walked or jumped at them they quickly retreated honking and complaining. Turkeys were the most stupid and spiteful of the lot. Always fighting amongst themselves or picking on the weakest in the flock to the point of stripping the victim of many feathers. Should it rain heavily, other poultry ran for shelter under a tree or other refuge but the turkeys just milled about the open in a blind panic, confused, gobbling franticly and getting thoroughly wet. The chicks of these flocks were a delight of course, either because of the way they looked or because of their comic behaviour.

22 THE OUTING

In the second full year of our evacuation, the Sunday school annual summer outing was revived having been cancelled the previous year because of the terrible uncertainties that the war had brought to the nation in 1940. We children had heard that special transport had been arranged to convey us to Shapwick railway station some two miles away on the moor. We were to travel from there to Burnham-on-Sea for the day. At 8:15 a.m. on the appointed day we assembled at the village crossroads where two construction lorries arrived. They were from the radio station being built on the parish hill and were of the open back, six-wheel type. Most children climbed on board but some older boys with bicycles had been told to ride ahead as there wasn't room for all. The few adult ladies, who were to accompany us, rode in the cabs with the drivers. By 8:30 a.m. both lorries moved off with their loads of excited, chattering children, through lower parish and past green fields over which a ground mist hung promising us a fine day. The road gently undulates for a mile before it meets the flatness of the moor forming part of the Somerset Levels. It was near the last rise that the lorries began to overtake our cycling companions whom we greeted with mild abuse and other comments when we saw them.

Both vehicles were then forced to slow to a crawl to pass through a herd of Farmer Tratt's cows being driven to pasture after milking. Edging through, our driver got clear just as Stan Jenkins riding his bike caught up with us. Reaching out his right hand he gripped the left-hand side of the tailboard of the lorry and, steering left-handed, went steadily along with us over the last rise and onto the straight road across the moor. We were all in a boisterous mood as the lorry jolted along and Stan remained with us smiling and enjoying his effortless ride. However, our driver began to accelerate and the vehicle steadily increased its speed. It was then that Stan should have let go but he didn't. Still chatting and joking with Stan we felt our speed increase further. A look of concern came over Stan's face as the lorry's speed reached the limit of his control of his bike. Ever faster we went and knowing that Stan was in real trouble, we urged him to let go. He was now very scared as we all thundered along and banter stopped. We must have been going at around fifty m.p.h. and realising that if his bike went from under him he would be killed, Stan let go. Now with both arms stiff as his hands gripped the handlebars he concentrated on steering, dropping rapidly behind and gradually slowing.

When about fifty yards behind we thought he was safe but then his bike gave a slight wobble quickly followed by a violent one. Stan was thrown headlong down the bank that supported the road above the general level of the marsh. We all laughed at what we thought a comical sight but our laughter died when he failed to rise. A few minutes later we drew up at the station's dusty forecourt to disembark, wondering if Stan was alright and talking anxiously to his younger brother David who had ridden with us in the lorry. After about ten minutes the second lorry arrived with the news that Stan was badly injured, seemingly with a broken arm and collarbone. An ambulance was summoned from the station to go to Stan. One of the ladies who was due to travel with us to Burnham waited with him at the scene of the accident, leaving us somewhat subdued at this setback at the start of our excursion. Then, standing on the station platform we looked down the single-track railway to see our steam train approaching and Stan was momentarily forgotten. Soon we were aboard the train and our spirits lifted again with chatter and horseplay resuming. Then we looked at David who sat with us quiet and downcast.

"Don't worry," we said, "Stan will be alright."

A David's eyes streamed with tears as he howled inconsolably.

Though the distance that we had to travel to Burnham was about ten miles, it took about an hour to get there because the train was slow and stopped at every station and halt along the way. Words of comfort and encouragement to David from one of our accompanying adults gradually settled him down as we at last steamed into our destination. We were eager to get on with the serious business of enjoying ourselves. Together we walked to a mission hall near the sea front where we stood outside to be instructed by an adult that we were to behave ourselves and to avoid getting into or causing trouble. We were also told that if in difficulties, where we could contact an adult. Finally, we were to report back to the mission hall at 5 p.m. sharp for tea, known to us as a bun-fight. We were then let loose on the town at around mid-morning. The sun was shining and for the first time in my life I was at the seaside free of the restraints from an adult. I am sure that this applied to most if not all of my companions and it felt good.

We quickly split up into small groups that we naturally formed in our free time back in the village. My four companions and I headed straight for the beach, running hard. As we neared the sands we saw the sea glittering in the distance. Being low tide the beach was enormous and the biggest I had ever seen. Though there were a few people about they sat in small knots and there was plenty of room for all. We continued our race to the water intent on paddling as we lacked swimming gear. So we entered the muddy waters of the Bristol Channel wading out to knee depth getting the legs of our short trousers wet, only to start larking about by splashing water around at each other and getting wetter still. It was wonderful but a pity that the water was so cold. After about thirty minutes we had had enough so back to the beach with the incoming tide. Sitting on the sands we took an early lunch of our sandwiches that had acquired a gritty texture from sand carried on a gentle breeze. We then set of at a trot to scour the town for its attractions.

We each carried pocket money; some sent from home, earnings from last summers' blackberry picking and a little from help with the harvest. I had the princely sum of eleven shillings and threepence (57new pence) having brought with me all of my ready cash. This amount was a little more than that the government gave Mrs. Stevens each week for my keep. Money went much further in those days but I was now at the seaside, on the loose and it was time to splash out. My companions were also in funds and the first delight we came across was an amusement kiosk. As part of a sweets and newsagents shop it was a small affair. Standing on its forecourt was a glass and painted metal cabinet around which we clustered. It contained a bed of thousands of small, sugar coated liquorice sweets on which rested about twenty or so valuable prizes all made of shiny, smooth metal and glass comprising small clocks, watches, cigarette lighters, etc. Overhanging this display within the cabinet was a small crane fitted with a grab, comprised of three highly polished chromium plated teeth. By careful alignment over a prize and with a penny inserted in to the machine's slot, the crane dropped its grab, closed it and resumed its former position after dropping anything that it had grabbed into a hopper that was accessible from outside when tilted open. The handsome prizes were a very effective lure but as they and the grab's surfaces were slippery, very few good prizes were dropped into the hopper. It seemed all that we were destined to win were a few of the liquorice sweets. It was a fascination though and we spent a few pennies on it but without real success.

We then went into the shop but there was not much of interest there so we returned to the machine. We could not resist a final go each so we took turns. When it was my turn the grab went down, missed and I had lost yet again. Then the crane developed a fault and repeated its programme of movements including dropping its grab at the prizes. I thought that my luck had changed and quickly manoeuvred the crane to a favourable position. Up and down it went missing again and again but at last securely lifting a wristwatch. This caused a roar of excitement from my companions and me. At the same time as I dived for the bin as the watch was dropped into it, I attempted to move the crane as it made yet another pass. My excitement and that of my mates was at fever pitch. As I reached the bin a boy, a total stranger, who had been standing among us held it shut and shouted "Mum", at the top of his voice. By now I was pushing him and trying to force his hands from the bin to get at my prize. The crane continued but only dropped sweets into the hopper as my mates twiddled the controls. "Mum, Mum", yelled the boy as I struggled with him and then "Mum" was among us. She had come from within the shop to her son and was obviously the proprietor. The boy blurted out an explanation of what had happened and she scolded us sharply and told us to clear off, ignoring my pleas for the watch. She produced a key, opened the cabinet and switched the power off. Only then did the crane cease its frantic activity. From a short distance we watched as an "Out of order" notice was fixed in place in the cabinet. Money lost, grumbling about the unfairness of the woman and dragging our feet, we walked sadly off, none sadder than myself.

Wandering further into the town centre we discovered an arcade with even bigger and better amusements. Entering, we saw that it was a virtual Aladdin's cave of exciting devices including plenty of pinball machines. Though we did not understand at the time, it was an efficient system for relieving us of our cash at a penny or ha'penny each go. Small change was not a problem as a woman, fat, blonde and irritable, who sat in a glass kiosk gave coppers in exchange for silver coins. Having spent freely on pinball we turned our attention to novelties requiring different levels of skill or none at all. Many of these were in small wall-cabinets operated by one ha'penny the incentive being if you won you received two coins in return. Some operated by a flip lever that catapulted a ball-bearing up in an attempt to get it to land in a series of small numbered cups under a covering of glass for payment. Six balls were allowed for each ha'penny but it was difficult to reach the required score for a payment. There were several variations on this theme in other machines.

We moved onto similar cabinets but each with a mechanical tableau hidden behind a small curtain. One was called, "English Execution", around which we crowded as a penny was inserted. The curtains jerkily parted to reveal a scene of model figures in a gloomy courtyard with a scaffold. The figures were about three inches high; several wearing forms of prison uniform common about seventy years earlier. Four figures placed centrally were different. One was a fully robed priest; another was the prison governor; the third a hangman with a hand on a lever and; the last, a prisoner with a noose around his neck standing on the scaffold's trapdoor. All figures were motionless, until with a whirr of mechanism the priest began to move a hand while his other moved a bible up and down as though giving the last rites. He suddenly stopped. Just as suddenly the governor moved a hand, the hangman pulled the lever, the prisoner fell through the trapdoor and the curtains snapped shut. This we found very comical and delighted in watching it perform several times. Some aspects that amused us were that all figures looked moth-eaten, the faces of all looked alike as though from the same family and suffering from some form of startled mental derangement. Then someone said, "Look, "French Execution", so we tried that. It was exactly the same except that the prisoner lay flat beneath the blade of a guillotine. When it fell, the prisoner's head dropped into a tiny basket, the curtains snapped shut as before but not quickly enough to prevent us from seeing the thin wire retracting the head ready for the next performance. We groaned at the near sameness of the other and moved on.

The next was tough guy stuff in the form of a "Test Your Strength" machine offering a kind of calliper brake handle similar to that of a bicycle. Within its cabinet was a disc numbered around its edge from nought to one hundred with a pointer. To one side of it was a card on which was a printed list of typical individuals in the population. About twenty were shown plus the average gripping power of each. A bank clerk's estimated scoring was twelve pounds, a sailor's seventy-five pounds and a farmer's eighty pounds were the ratings, the last being the best of all. This fitted nicely into our perception of these individuals. We each spent several pennies at the grip trying to prove that we were all future farmers.

Then we were off to the rifle range. It was unusual, having one rifle fixed to pivot and pointing at a small illuminated screen. When a penny was inserted, a target appeared on the screen. Taking careful aim, I squeezed the trigger and a bullet hole appeared on the target's outer ring. Proof of aim was delivered at the rifle's base in the form of a small square of celluloid film with a pinhole through the outer ring of the target. My attempt resulted in derisive remarks from my mates who then took their turns with similar results. After several goes we found that by aiming off the bulls-eye we got better results and that the pin mechanism was misaligned. We felt cheated but it was, of course a part of the psychology employed by arcades to induce customers to try several times to prove what good shots they were.

It so happened that it was "Wings for Victory Week" in Burnham starting on the day we had arrived. It was one of a series of fund-raising war exhibits typical of many others touring our towns and cities to finance warplanes. These displays appealed to the people's patriotic feelings of the time. Walking from the arcade we trod a route not previously known to us and in the distance saw Spitfire and Hurricane aircraft. One of each was parked on a paved area on the seafront so we broke into a run so we would not waste a moment before we got to them. People were allowed to sit in the cockpits of these fighter planes but when we got to them there were long queues of adults and children waiting their turn. The entrance fee was the purchase of a sixpence. (two and a half new pence) National Savings stamp. Mounted on a wooden trestle nearby lay a one thousand pound. bomb (just the casing really but we thought it real) with its fin. As we purchased our stamps we were told by a bored aircraftsman to stick them onto the bomb on which there were already hundreds of others. He then varnished over them with a brush he held so they could not be taken off and reused. On the side of the bomb was written in chalk, "This one's for you Adolf", and this pleased us very much as we imagined that when it was dropped on Hitler we would have added to its impact however minutely. Everything was an illusion as not only was the bomb a dummy, so were the fighter planes but they were all real to us. After a long wait in the queue we took turns to climb a short ladder into one or other of the cockpit seats. Our visit there was but brief but we were able to look through the cannon sights, hold the joystick and press the firing button (no bullets or sound of course). Our imaginations ran riot as we shot enemy planes out of the sky. This experience was the highlight of the day.

Money that we had remaining was now short. Having eaten our packed sandwiches early we were now famished so spent a little on some currant buns that were dry and difficult to swallow. It was about mid-afternoon so we returned to the beach but this time explored its westerly end. The tide had been in and now was well on its way out again. As we walked over the damp sand we felt our feet sinking in a few centimetres and this frightened us as we had heard of quicksand and of its dangers. As an adult I was sure that the beach at Burnham did not have them but at the time we boys decided not to take any chances (I have since learned that lives have been lost there in quicksand). Returning inland, we discovered a fun fair off the sea front on an area of waste ground and there spent some more time and money on the dodgems and side stalls. Try as we might to have something to show for our money, we never won a coconut or other prize but while it lasted we enjoyed ourselves. However, the situation with our funds was getting desperate. We had been spending like drunken sailors ashore. Having started out with the most, I was down to just a few coppers. So too were my mates. There was only one thing that we could do; win some more on the "Roll a Penny" stall. Five minutes later we were all flat broke! We wandered glumly around the fair looking at the various things that we could not afford to go on or try.

Then hunger pangs told us that 5 p.m. was near and so was the promised bun-fight. Returning to the town at a trot we arrived at the door with about fifteen minutes to spare looking decidedly more dishevelled than when we were last there. Joining the somewhat disorderly queue we did our share in the general pushing and shoving, arguments, laughter and calling out to the girls. Then the doors were opened and we all rushed into the hall many of those at the back overtaking others at the front. Over the long benches set against rows of trestle tables we went in a scramble for the best seats and so that mates could all sit together. Tables had been laid with cakes, buns, sandwiches and the like and soft drinks too. We were served and supervised by women in frocks some of whom were those who had accompanied us from the village. Whilst all of the arguments over reserved places and who was sitting with whom were being settled we were called on by the ladies to be quiet. As the din subsided our gaze concentrated upon the platters of food set before us. Before our grubby hands could reach for it we were called upon to stand for grace. Because we had not seen him all day we were surprised to hear the voice of our vicar intoning that we should be grateful for the feast before us. As the "Amen" was spoken, we sat down and hands shot out to the food as a general hubbub of chatter began. Food rationing must have made things difficult for those arranging bun-fights like the one that day but we did well, not least because it ended with helpings of custard, jelly and blancmange. With tables and floor littered with our debris we were told that we would leave for the train from outside the mission hall at 7.30 p.m. so we still had one and a half hours to ourselves. The final surprise came as we filed out of the door and into the street. Our vicar pink and beaming shyly gave each of us a shilling for, "Personal spending" We were solvent again!

Where to go? There was only one place. Clutching our shillings we returned to the fun fair. Unable to resist the attractions it wasn't long before our shillings too were spent. Straggling to the mission at the appointed time we were marshalled into a double line and walked to the railway station tired but happy. At Shapwick station, tractors and trailers waited to return us to the village. A few days later the sequel to this day hit home for me. It was time to write home to Mum and

Dad and having written my letter and addressed it, I did not have one and a half pence to buy a postage stamp. Rather shamefacedly I approached Mrs. Stevens for a loan of this amount. Surprised or even shocked, she said,

"What? You've spent all your money and nothing's left?"

"Yes," I replied.

"Well," said she, "I'm not lending money to you, you naughty boy, and let that be a lesson to you. You will have to ask your mum and dad for some."

The question that crossed my mind was, "How can I ask my parents for cash when I can't send a letter?" When Granny Moxey heard about reckless spending she looked at me with a big smile on her face and said,

"What Ted? Did you eat it all?"

I was in a fix but then I remembered that at my pending departure from Dagenham my dad gave me some advice. He said that if ever I needed to send a letter home and had no money I should write in the place where a stamp would be fixed these words, "From an evacuated child". This is what I did and the letter got through without a surcharge. Though I thought it harsh at the time, the decision by Mrs. Stevens was the right one. I think that ever since I have never been "stony broke" but that isn't to say I was never hard up at times. The lesson I had that day seems to have been learned.

23 HARVEST

Depending on the weather, July and August were the months for harvesting cereals, usually wheat. Drier and dustier to handle than hay it followed a similar work pattern. On a hot day if one stood at the edge of a field of ripened wheat, popping sounds could be heard as the heat caused the ears to split. Gathering the crop involved a marvellous reaping machine of the time. This not only cut the crop but also caught it as it fell, bundled it into sheaves of equal size tying each firmly with twine and then discharged each in succession to one side in rows around the field. Though now superceded by the more sophisticated combine harvester, this horse drawn reaper was ingenious and fascinating to watch. The sheaves were then collected in pairs by hand, placed butt down and upright in stooks (double rows) in sets of ten or more to shed any rain that might arrive before they were loaded onto wagons and taken to a farmyard for stacking. The work was hard but enjoyable with the minor hazard of harvest mites. These near invisible creatures burrowed under the surface of skin and cause itchy, red spots. When I had them I thought that I had been infected with chicken pox. After a week or two the spots disappeared so apart from a lot of scratching, it wasn't more than just a nuisance.

Aspects of harvesting were very similar to those of haymaking such as dryness of crop, haulage, stacking, etc. If stacked damp the grain would smell musty and even sprout its value being much reduced. Judging ripeness was also important for if left standing and over ripe, much grain was shed and so lost. Bad weather was feared and for this reason skies were anxiously watched. Though all of the farms in the district were dairy each had some areas sown to wheat, oats or barley and much of this was as directed by the government in the drive for food production. Loading the wagons was another skilled job as the sheaves had to be laid in an interlocking system otherwise they slipped from the load. This also applied when the stack, called a mow, was being built. The first time I was involved in this work was at the Limekiln, the furthest field of the group farmed by Mr. Stevens. It is next to and slopes down to Combe Bottom. It was a lovely day and the work was going well and two loads were soon ready to haul away. Pleasant the mare was led by a man at her head as she pulled the lead wagon. As it passed through the gate and onto the road one front wheel slipped into the roadside ditch causing the load to suddenly bear down on the mare's hindquarters. She could be seen straining to hold it as her legs bent. After a moment her legs straightened as she managed to steady the load but the wagon was stuck blocking the gate.

Squeezing past the wagon through the gate the other men came to the horse to see the problem. One climbed onto the load and passed sheaves down to lighten the front of the wagon. Judged to be light enough and with the men pushing, the mare heaved again and onto the road then rolled wagon and all. A quick reloading and we were on our way. When we got to the Limekiln where the road drops steeply, a heavy metal "shoe" hanging from a chain fixed to the wagon was slipped beneath a rear wheel. As the wheel passed onto it, the chain became taut and this had the effect of a brake, locking the wheel as the metal shoe skidded down the hill. A simple but very effective way of stopping runaway loads!

Loads were built into a stack in a paddock next to the rickyard in a manner very similar to the hay. The big difference was that the sheaves were laid in an interlocking pattern as on the wagon, as the stack was progressively built with the outermost sheaves laid with their butts outwards. The straw forming sheaves was shiny and smooth and being so, they sometimes slipped to create a bulge on the side of the stack that threatened collapse of the whole. If this happened the bulge had to be supported by a heavy timber prop. Once the field had been harvested it was a common practice among farmers to haul their chickens in their coops to the cleared fields for the birds to be let out onto the stubble. Thus spilt grain went to fatten the chickens. There was one disadvantage to this temporary measure, which was that a visit had to be made at the start and end of each day to open and close the coop so that the birds inside were safe from a hungry fox overnight.

One aspect of harvesting cereals was the sport that occurred as the reaper circled the field, cutting the crop from the boundaries inwards. As the stand of uncut cereal gradually diminished in area, some of its wild inhabitants would make a dash for safety. They had been using the crop as a well-stocked larder but now had been forced to retreat to the field centre as their cover was cut down. The first was likely to be a covey of partridges that burst up suddenly with a whirr of wings to fly and then glide to safety into the next field. Being protected game birds they were safe from us. However, the rabbits there were fair game for men and boys waiting for them in a sparse circle some yards within and around the field perimeter. Most farmers allowed anyone who wished to try their luck in bagging one or two of these. By keeping an eye on the progress of the reaper, villagers would know when to arrive to take their chance. Upwards of twenty might be present; some men carrying shotguns, others with dogs and the rest, including boys, were armed with sticks or stones. When the area of uncut wheat was only a few yards in diameter, rabbits broke cover, usually one at a time to race for shelter in a boundary hedge. The distance could be anything up to, say, eighty yards and both speed and luck played an important part for both pursued and pursuer. As a rabbit emerged at full speed, shouts arose from boys and men and fingers pointed to it. If anyone with a shotgun with an unobstructed field of fire was within range, then the creature was as good as dead. If no gun was there or people were in the way, then the terrified creature had to elude sticks, stones and pursuing dogs. The odds were a bit more in the rabbit's favour in those circumstances. Sometimes a fleet-footed dog overtook a rabbit and after some frantic dodging about by both, the dog could take it. More rarely a rabbit would fall victim to a stick or stone.

I joined in this activity one evening at one of Manor Farm's fields. I had a stick about one and a half yards long. It was curved so when brought down, about twelve inches struck the ground thus allowing a greater margin for error when striking. A number of rabbits had run for safety and most had got through. Then another appeared, going away from where I stood only to suddenly change direction to head straight at me. I had plenty of time to raise the stick above my head, poised to bring it down at the right instant and concentrating my gaze upon it as it rushed, bobbing, to me. At the precise moment for a hit, I brought the stick down hard only to hit a black dog a glancing blow on its side as it suddenly appeared from the left, intent on the rabbit. The rabbit ran between my legs to the safety of the hedge as the dog yelped to fall in a heap, then rise and return to its master giving me a reproachful look as he went.

The most remarkable kill that I ever saw was in Farmer Tucker's wheat field off of the back lane to Ashcott. Bob Grogan, Hoppy Hopkins and I were there having wandered in as the rabbits were running. This large field had been worked for a day or two; so many sheaves had been stooked at the end of each day of reaping, with now more standing wheat being cut. Then we saw a fleeing rabbit heading in our direction. Seeing us it decided that its best chance lay in the shelter of a stook, which it entered with a rustling thump. It was nearby so keeping our eyes fixed on it we took up some stones and encircled the stook. Bob started to dismantle it but had hardly begun when out sped the rabbit, its white scut (tail) showing, followed by a hail of stones. Hoppy had taken steadier aim with a flat stone that he loosed at the rabbit as all others fell wide of the mark. His stone sped along gliding just above the stubble. Catching the rabbit up, it struck a sharp blow behind its ears causing it to somersault over to lay dead. A whoop of triumph arose from us all and the rabbit was quickly snatched up and handed to Hoppy as we congratulated him. When it was held up by its hind legs we regarded it with pride because of our success and we also admired Hoppy's accuracy with the stone. Farmer Tucker was near the field centre and we went to show him our trophy. As we came near he looked up from his work to say,

"What have thee got thar then?"

Excitedly, we told him how the perfect stone throw had felled it.

"Let I have a look at 'un then," exclaimed the man and Hoppy passed it to him. Farmer Tucker's face took on a crafty smirk as he said,

"My field, my rabbit," and deaf to our protestations, turned on his heel and stamped off with it. Poor Hoppy was downcast at being deprived of his kill but took comfort in the way it had been done. We others heaped more praise on him and for days after described the throw in graphic detail to those who had not been present.

24 CIDER

The majority of the apple trees in the village orchards bore cider apples and most farmers made their own brew. When the crop was ripe, apples were collected either by being knocked from the trees with sticks or as windfalls. The care taken when collecting desert apples was abandoned for the sharp and sour cider apples. Bagged in jute sacks they were carted off to a farm that had a press. Mr. Stevens' co-operator farmer, Mr. Jennings, had one of these and that was where Old Farm's cider was made. There the apples were coarsely pulped and stacked in layers approximately six inches deep alternating with a two inch layer of clean wheat straw to hold it in place on the press base, rather like bricks and mortar are bound together. These layers were built into what was called a "cheese" about a yard square and of the same height. A thick, heavy board was then placed on top and the block of the press was lowered onto it. Fitting a pole into a slot above a strong wooden screw, it was turned as you would a capstan, forcing the block down hard onto the cheese. From the pulpy mass gushed a sweet, scented, brownish-red juice that coursed into an encircling channel to run to an outlet that spilled through a fine mesh sieve and into a small barrel. We children quickly learned to find a straight straw though which to suck up some of this juice from the channel. It was deliciously sweet despite it coming from sharp tasting apples and we thoroughly enjoyed ourselves. We would have done this for hours had an old farm worker not said,

"If thee young-uns don't give that a rest thee'll be on the midden fur a fortnight."

The cider cheese was built up again and again with pulp using the original pressing as a base and re-pressed each build. As the vertical sides of the cheese grew it was occasionally trimmed with a hay knife, the trimmings then placed on top of the cheese before more pressing. This left its sides smooth and solid looking, becoming black from exposure to air. As more cider flowed, dozens of wasps and some flies were attracted. They swarmed over the cheese enjoying the sweet juice. Though the cider was new and unfermented these insects were soon drunk. Some wasps wandered off over the timbers of the press while others kept climbing up the surface of the cheese only to fall off to be swept along the channel by the flow and before going into the barrel caught in the fine mesh sieve. Others flew erratically about the room and it was those we had to be wary of. They were as some of their human counterparts were when drunk, ill tempered, nasty and prone to violence. When the small barrel was almost full another replaced it and so the process was repeated until pressing was complete. As for the cheese, after a couple of days when it was no longer running with juice the press was wound up to reveal the block of pulp looking like a very dark and huge, compressed bread pudding with a similar texture. It was then carted to pasture at milking time, spread on the grass for the cows that needed no encouragement to eat it.

The small cider barrels were taken to the cellar at Old Farm and decanted into large ones that had once held earlier vintages, their interiors having earlier been scrubbed clean by Mr. Stevens. The large barrels of new cider were visited regularly by Mr. Stevens who monitored their progress as they turned to real alcoholic cider. The barrels each had a bunghole at its top over which a bung was laid loosely and not driven in, allowing the liquid to ferment without building up pressure in the barrel. Through the bunghole came bubbling and gurgling as fermentation continued, easing after a few weeks when the bung was rammed into place. These barrels were left to mature their contents to the following year when it could be drunk. Some barrels in the cellar contained cider a few years old. The older the cider the paler it became. Old cider was very sharp to the taste and as far as I could tell was only favoured by a few men and some of them gasped and sucked their teeth when they tasted it.

21 Frank Crann, Ted and Norman

25 FREE FRUIT

The village children showed us how to do a little browsing on wild strawberries on our walks in the summers and in autumns, on hazelnuts. Though the former were quite difficult to find and tiny, they were delicious. We also sought beech mast but though seemingly there were many of these nuts beneath the trees, we found they were mostly empty husks so not worth too much searching. One of the last of the autumnal activities was blackberry picking which we children and several village women did for pocket or pin money. The berries were sold at threepence. (one and a quarter new pence) per pound, that being the mid-war price bought by Mrs. Argent who acted as an agent for a fruit/jam company. She lived in a cottage that bordered on the Croft meadow in Back Lane. This activity set me up with funds for Christmas, and allowed me to buy a few modest presents for Mum back home in Dagenham. Most of the best places for picking were well known to the villagers but visits to outlying fields when bringing the cows home for milking sometimes led to the discovery of a secret crop on hedges unknown to others. September evenings stayed light until about 8:30 p.m. in the war so it was possible to slip off with a large basket after school and teatime to gather the berries. Another essential tool was a crook stick with which to hook down berries that were otherwise out of reach.

I once discovered an abundant crop at Combe Bottom where a hedge, cut and re-laid the previous winter, had new bramble shoots heavily laden with fruit. There were hundreds of them, many an inch in diameter and their scent hung in the still evening air. The only problem was that a dry ditch had been cleared and re-shaped in front of the hedge. By standing in the ditch I could pick low berries but to reach those higher required me to straddle it with a foot on each bank as though attempting the splits. Despite my ungainly progress down the hedgerow and the failing light I set a personal record that evening with about 15 lbs. picked in little more than 30 minutes. As dusk fell I found that ripe and unripe berries all seemed black so I had to finish my work. Walking back with my brimming basket I felt happy and thrilled at the prospect of around three shillings and sixpence. earned when I got to Mrs. Argent. She was always ready at anytime to buy and a knock at her door would bring her quickly to it. She was a motherly woman, dark haired, bright-eyed, smiling with a friendly manner. The berries were weighed on her spring scales and money paid before the blackberries were emptied into a tub, one of many in her lean-to outhouse, some full and others awaiting more of the season's crop. It was a nice place to visit for she was always cheerful with a friendly word to all. Because of a shortage of fruit rich in vitamin C, there was a demand for rose hips that we gathered from hedgerow dog roses. I understood that somewhere, these were rendered into bottles of rose-hip syrup intended via mothers for babies and young children. This was all part of the war effort in the absence of oranges etc.

Another autumn crop as a source of pocket money was the wild field mushroom gathered at first light from pastures. This was not as popular as blackberrying because of the early start entailed and the uncertainty of how the weather was going to be. There was always the consideration whether a mushroom picker in someone else's field might not be welcome in the owner's eyes especially if they were anticipated for their own breakfast. I could never rouse myself from my warm bed at such an unearthly hour but Norman did and for several days returned home with baskets of the fungi. They varied in size from buttons to the so-called "horse mushrooms", about one foot diameter. The other problem was getting them to Bridgwater market whilst they were fresh but Mr. Stevens often went each week at that time of year so that solved the problem.

26 AUTUMN/WINTER

The first main job on the farm was hedging and ditching, starting in November and continuing intermittently as conditions allowed until all were in good condition. Not all hedges were worked on but phased in a sequence over the years and then only those becoming overgrown or thin at the base. The work of cutting and laying a hedge to around five feet high was very skilled. Properly done it was a source of craftsman pride. Moreover, a farm with well maintained hedges was an indication of a good farmer The main objective was ensure that hedges were finished in such a way to thicken their lower growth to provide a dense stock-proof barrier. Upright stems as thick as a man's arm were cut two-thirds through near the base with a billhook and bent in line with the hedge almost horizontally; thus ensuring a flow of sap was maintained. This encouraged shoots to sprout along its length in spring to thicken the hedge. Some tree saplings growing in the hedge were selected for growing on to maturity where appropriately sited. As the hedge was laid note was taken of any rabbit warrens within it that looked promising for further investigation another day.

This work produced a large amount of brushwood some of which was taken back to the farmhouse for kindling wood. There was a large surplus however, and this and other growth from the hedging was burnt on fires built successively along the edge of the field as the work progressed. This was the job that Norman, Bob Grogan and I thoroughly enjoyed as the fires were big and in cold weather were cosy to be near. One of the men lit a fire and got it going well and using pitchforks, together they got behind a line of brushwood and rolled it as a bundle about six feet high onto the blaze. Having seen how it was done we three took on the job whilst the men worked on the hedge. Sparks shot skywards as the fire took hold of the fresh fuel as we rolled successive bundles onto it. It was the best job in an open field on a cold winter's day.

Some of the hard work on the farm was relieved by the sport of ferreting that also provided food for the table. Mr. Stevens kept a white ferret, a kind of polecat, in a hutch within a lean-to in the farmyard. Like others of its kind it had a stench of its own probably because it was a carnivore living only on raw flesh. When someone fed it, it was on its food in a flash and one had to be quick to drop the food otherwise it could mistakenly give a finger or hand a vicious bite in its eagerness. On one dry winter's day Mr. Stevens, Jack Exon and me went ferreting. The ferret was taken from its hutch and put in a sack and carried to a warren in one of Old Farm's fields at Combe Bottom at the edge of the parish. It was a lovely winter's day, calm and sunny with the scent of earth and dry grass as we set to work. The first warren had several exits so pegs fixed a net over each. The ferret was then fitted with a collar on the end of a long line and as one net was lifted slightly, it was popped into the rabbit hole. It was quickly gone from sight and the line was paid out as the ferret went deep into the warren. Suddenly a rabbit shot from an exit only to be immediately enmeshed, grabbed, freed and its neck broken by a punch behind its ears. The net was quickly replaced in case a second rabbit emerged. After a wait for other rabbits and if no more came, the ferret was withdrawn from the hole and then inserted into another nearby followed by more rabbits rushing out to be trapped and killed as before. Moving onto another warren the same procedure was followed but though the ferret disappeared into a hole no rabbits were flushed out. Jack said,

"Bide quiet a minute." We all listened intently. "Dost thee hear that?" he asked but we others heard nothing.

Lying on the grass over the warren, Jack pressed his ear to the ground to listen again.

"He be stopped there," he said, meaning the ferret, "he be up to summat." Pulling on the line, the ferret was withdrawn to appear licking its bloody jaws. "I told thee so," Jack said and taking up a spade he had brought, he began to dig a hole at the spot where he had lain to listen. Carefully working, he reached the burrow made by rabbits and exposed the hindquarters of one, pulled it free by its hind legs and killed it. Reaching along the tunnel again he gripped the hind legs of another, withdrew it and killed that also. He then held up the first and we saw that the creature's head was bloody. Further investigation of the burrow revealed that a large jutting stone partly blocked it, halting the second rabbit to be taken out. Its companion behind was trapped at the mercy of the ferret. The ferret had climbed along the unfortunate rabbit's back, starting with its eye had begun to eat it alive. Jack's sharp hearing had heard the rabbit's shrieks underground. Hardened though we were to catching and killing rabbits to eat, we winced at the thought of how the poor rabbit had suffered. It was horrible to contemplate and silenced us for a while.

Shooting rabbits was another autumn and winter activity for farmers and some other men in the village who owned shotguns. Their kills also supplemented scarce meat rations, especially those men not employed in agriculture. Shooting with twelve bore shotguns usually took place on a Saturday but also during some lighter evenings. I once pointed out to Mr. Stevens a rabbit sitting up at about thirty yards distance when dusk was gathering. He stalked getting closer and closer but before he took aim he peered hard once more only to then lower his gun. My rabbit turned out to be a dried thistle! The only other way of getting a rabbit for the pot was by the use of snares set in field margins and placed over the route of a rabbit run. These runs were easily seen amongst grass not cropped short. The steps of rabbit along it clearly showed regularly in the grass as small flattened patches. The snares were simple devices comprising of a running noose of stranded, twisted brass wire about twenty inches long, attached to a cord at its end. The cord was pegged firmly into the ground with the noose set open over a rabbit run. Positioned between two patches of footmarks, the noose was supported by a short, straight, slender stick, slightly split at its top to receive the wire. The head of a rabbit hopping along the run entered the noose and with its next hop the noose tightened around its neck from which there was no escape.

It was essential that snares set the evening before were checked the following morning to ensure that any rabbits ensnared were found, killed and collected otherwise they could die a long and painful death. One cold, misty and frosty morning I went with Bob

Grogan to check snares at the Lime Kiln. There was a haunted atmosphere in the countryside on such early mornings as everything lay still and hushed. Our boots clunked on the iron-hard frozen ground as we walked, trees were made faint by the mist and our breath hung in the air. A rabbit was snared overnight and releasing it, I broke its neck in the usual way and reset the snare. It was the first animal I had ever killed.

One farmer, Mr. Tucker, was lax in this snare checking. When roaming over fields including one of his of an evening, we found a dead rabbit in a snare belonging to him. It had lain there for some days and had partly dried. There were seven boys present at the time and none resisted the temptation to steal it to roast in a nearby copse. Whilst the others collected kindling and other wood I gutted and skinned the rabbit, cut two forked sticks and a crossbar from a hedge to make a roasting frame in the traditional campfire way. Placing the kindling beneath this we got a small fire going and when well alight and the smoke had died down, hung the rabbit over the flames to cook.

We sat on the ground in a circle around the fire waiting for our feast to be ready, watching it intently. After about ten minutes we were getting bored and gave the carcass a poke to see if it was tender. It wasn't. After an interminable twenty minutes more we decided it must be ready. Wrenching off bits of the rabbit we began to chew the warm half-raw, stringy and tough flesh. After two or three more bites and chewing, we gave up, as it wasn't like home cooking. Kicking the fire out we all went home. In the early evening on the day following whilst I was sitting in the inglenook reading a book, Norman burst excitedly into the room and announced, "Some boys have stolen a rabbit and Major Royle is down at the village giving them a telling off". There was no mention of my involvement and I adopted an air of calm interest despite the lump in my throat and the knot in my stomach. Next day I heard from my mates that a seven-year-old boy who had accompanied us had blurted out our adventure to the lady with whom he was living. She had told the neighbours about it and Major Royle was informed, as unofficial judge and jury, to deal with the matter. I got off Scot-free but we were all fed up with the informant not least because we ordinarily would not have allowed him to be with us as he was just a kid.

One day Bob Grogan and I went searching for a rabbit's nest and found one against a hedge. We knew our find was likely to have young ones in as the doe had earthed up the entrance to the burrow before she left to feed. Scraping the earth away we reached in to feel a nest of fur and several tiny rabbits. Withdrawing one, we saw that it was blind and naked. Replacing it, we felt around the short burrow to discover that it formed a small round chamber at its end – all very cosy and comfortable. Having satisfied our curiosity we re-blocked the entrance with earth and left. It was a delightful thing to have experienced.

Life on the farm in winter slowed to some extent but with the persisting routine tasks of milking and feeding of cows, calves, horses and chickens. When the weather was harsh with frosts, snow or prolonged rain the cows and horses were kept in their stalls or stables. There they were fed with hay, mangolds and cattle cake. Cutting hay from the hayrick with a big hay-knife was a job I enjoyed, working down a column of cut hay. It was then lifted off in a thick wad and carried to the cows and their mangers The only hazard with this was when a wad was lifted a hand could hold a thistle cut with the hay. The spines were even nastier than usual as they were unseen and being dry, sharper than ever. After the cows had been confined to their stalls for a week or more due to severe weather and then released into a field, some seemed overjoyed to be free. They rushed off cavorting in a clumsy gamboling way, tails up, udders swinging as they bounded awkwardly over the grass. They couldn't keep that up for long but having done it, they seemed pleased with themselves.

27 GIRLS

As we boys grew older our interest in the school's girl pupils also grew and there was competition to win one of them as "his girl". Josephine (Josie) Howe (Frizzy Lizzie as Granny Moxey called her because of her cloud of fair hair), Betty Ayres and one or two others were the most popular. I fell for Betty who at the age of twelve was coltish, dark-haired, dark-eyed and pretty with a nice smile. I asked my friend Bob to tell her that I liked her at which news her complexion turned a delicate shade in a pink blush and caused her to giggle. Later, I wrote to her as follows, "Dear Betty, will you be my girl. I like you, Love Ted x x". Though I did not get a written reply I was accepted and so we were recognised as going out together though in fact we never went out together alone but occasionally talked when we were with other children. I strengthened her favour towards me by sending, via another girl, two pieces of "Sharps Toffee", a kind of stick-jaw. This gift represented a great sacrifice on my part in those days of sweet rationing. A little later I was a bit surprised to see that both were chewing and realised that Betty had shared my gift with the other girl which wasn't my intent. This friendship was all rather shy and innocent and we never kissed.

This went on for a few weeks until our class was in a field playing rounders under the supervision of our teacher, Mr. King. Betty and I were on opposing sides and when it was her turn to bat she struck the ball in my direction and instinctively I caught it and she was out. I immediately sensed that my catch might not be very well received but though seeming a little surprised, Betty smiled at me and after the game spoke to me in her usual friendly way. All seemed well. A little later Bob Grogan said that he thought I was wrong to have caught her ball causing my sense of foreboding to grow. The next day, Betty was cold and distant towards me, and that was the end of that phase of her being "My girl". Some weeks later we got back together again for a time but it was never the same and a cynical thought crossed my mind that she only wanted my toffee.

Other girls appeared on the scene who were visiting relatives at Shapwick. We took a greater or lesser interest in these according to how pretty they were unless they were "good sports". The latter girls were ones that could match the exploits of boys in climbing trees, running, etc. One of them came with her brother to an outlying farm for a summer holiday where Bob Grogan and I spent several happy times exploring the farm buildings with them. She was definitely the "Tom-boy" type being strong and lithe. She surprised Bob and me one day when she wanted to pee. Instead of squatting, as did other girls of our acquaintance, she lowered her knickers, freed a foot and raised a knee to lean it against a wall. With legs spread, she did a reasonable imitation of a boy's technique in similar circumstances.

During the summer of 1942 the twelve year-old schoolgirl sister of the replacement teacher who arrived that year, came to stay with her for the summer holidays. Amazingly, she let it be known that she liked me and so became my girlfriend for a few weeks. It was the usual awkward innocent friendship but I did wonder at the time if she had told her sister and what did she make of us. After the holiday period the girl left never to return. Her teacher sister left later at the beginning of 1943. Another of my girlfriends was Iris from West Ham. She and several of us boys spent hours building camp dwellings out of branches in woods and copses and sometimes included a roof made from a corrugated iron sheet. We even provided makeshift soft furnishings out of hay to resemble armchairs and sofas. Iris's piece de resistance comedy act was what she called a drawer dance. She would drop her knickers to her ankles and then dance up and down on the spot to make us boys laugh.

The arrival of one little girl marked a joyful occasion at Old Farm when Marjorie was born on 21st, of March 1943 at Butleigh Maternity Hospital to Mr. and Mrs. Stevens. Norman and I had begun to notice the changed appearance of Mrs. Stevens weeks earlier but nothing was said between us or by anyone else – at least within my earshot. As the weeks passed so it became clear that she was soon to have the baby though still nothing was openly said. Then about mid-March on a bright spring afternoon I saw her on her hands and knees in the kitchen, vigorously scrubbing the large random flagstones with soap and water, an activity that Granny came to remark upon with some surprise. That evening came and the house followed its usual routine and continued the next day, but the same evening Mrs. Stevens had gone but still nothing was said. When Norman came home from school I met him as he entered the kitchen. We looked at each other, each knowing what the other was thinking. Those thoughts that had gone unspoken between us suddenly became a tension that suddenly broke and we chuckled with relief. We were told later that Mrs. Stevens had had a baby girl who was to be called Marjorie and that Mr. Stevens was to visit wife and baby the following morning.

When I got home to the farm that afternoon there was an air of excitement and Mr. Stevens and Granny were especially happy, speaking of the baby saying all was well with both her and mother. A day or so later Mr. Stevens happened to invite me to take a ride with him in the butchers van making deliveries in nearby villages. Calling at a cottage near Pedwell, he was asked by a lady how Alice was and cheerfully answered, "We have a little maid." This seemed to me a lovely and unusual way to tell of a new baby and a manner of speaking about it that I had never heard before or since.

Naturally, the arrival of Marjorie became the main topic of conversation among the wider family and especially among the aunts. Over ensuing days, Mr. Stevens took family members to the hospital to see both mother and child as both remained there for two weeks. One day Mr. Stevens asked if I would like to go to which I answered, "Yes please". Later that day in conversation with Auntie Nellie I heard Granny muttering in a troubled tone,

"Why does Herbert want to take him? He's not a member of the family."

But I did go to see Mrs. Stevens who was sitting up in bed wearing a bed jacket and looking bright and well. After a while I was taken to a glass screen along a corridor to see Marjorie though it was difficult to know which cot she was in as the ward seemed to be full of them.

After two weeks both returned to the farm and a new daily routine of attending to baby's needs was added to the usual domestic activities. It was all new to me. Later when my parents came for a short visit, Mrs. Stevens remarked to them that I had taken a keen interest in Marjorie. Until that was said, my attitude was one which I was not aware was unusual and was something that had happened, I suppose, quite naturally. It must have been so because during that conversation I asked my mum and dad, "Why can't we have another baby?" at which the adults exchanged knowing glances but no further comment came. I wonder why!

The most startling of all of the girls was Millie. One autumn afternoon I was passing a cottage, outside of which stood a fellow evacuee of about my age. He was in a slight state of nervous agitation and seemed to be anxiously looking up and down the lane.

"What's the matter?" I asked.

"Go in and see what's on our kitchen table," he replied. Slipping along a side passage to the rear garden I met another lad who raised the back door latch to show me into a kitchen made dim by curtains being partly drawn over a window. Two other boys were in the room and as my eyes became accustomed to its gloom, I saw Millie. She was lying on her side on the kitchen table; her head propped up from the elbow by one hand. She was smiling gently and looking interestedly at me. It was then that I noticed that her knickers were down at her knees and her skirt up to her navel revealing at the top of her legs a dark triangle against the whiteness of her thighs. This sight came as a stunning surprise to me and as I stared, I had a feeling not only of excitement but also sickness in the pit of my stomach. At long last! This was what I had heard so many boys talk about so much.

"Touch it," a voice said. Trembling, my hand reached out to feel the warm, crisp, dark hair.

The effect that this had on me was electric, and a fierce arousal took over my loins. Though I was aware of the biological essentials, I was unprepared for the situation and did not know how to cope with it. Gazing awhile at this wonderful sight I was then gripped with fear of discovery by an adult. Making my excuses, I hurried out scuttling home with a certain difficulty of movement because of my raging arousal. Fortunately, no-one was about when I got indoors as my agitated behaviour would have given me away as being up to something forbidden. Grabbing a book, I opened it and sat on a settle in the inglenook. Staring at the page, my mind could not concentrate on any of the words that met my eyes. All that I was aware of was the thrilling sight just seen and the arousal that would not go away. It was with great difficulty that I was able to speak and act normally when adult members of the household eventually came and went from the room. It was about forty-five minutes later that I could stand up with reasonably certainty that a part of my anatomy would not give an indication as to what my thoughts remained concentrated upon. Millie remained a popular girl with us admirers who occasionally displayed her ample bosom to us.

28 WAR IN SHAPWICK

Though safe in Somerset I was very aware of the progress of the war through news bulletins broadcast by the BBC and newspapers. Seeing me sitting in the kitchen reading the "Daily Mail" was a source of comment by Mrs. Stevens as she thought it unusual for a child to be so engrossed. Listening to the victory of the German army over France and the evacuation of our troops at Dunkirk made me think things were getting desperate for Britain. Hearing the news bulletins at that time I was surprised and somewhat baffled by the way the evacuation was being described as a triumph. Amazing though it was that so many of our soldiers were rescued in the way they were, the term "triumph" didn't ring true in my ears and I was worried as so many others must have been. Of course these broadcasts were putting a gloss on the news in an attempt to sustain morale; a propaganda ploy that I didn't understand at the time.

The only concession to the risk of air raids on the village (a very unlikely event) was the construction of a brick blast-wall in front of each of the main entrances to the school building. If there was an air raid warning, the cloakroom lobbies at these entrances were where we pupils assembled to sit on the floor with our backs to the walls. The only indication of a warning was from sirens in either Bridgwater or Street, respectively nine or five miles away. There must have been many warnings that went un-noticed because of the distances involved; the fact that instruction from the teacher would blot out the faint siren sound; and that certain wind directions could carry the sound away. On a few occasions a pupil would call to the teacher,

"Air raid warning Sir", at which he listened to then tell the class to go to the lobby with our gas masks. These warnings had the advantage of a chance to skip a lesson but the disadvantage of feeling under attack. At times in the lobby, we practiced putting on our gas masks that we found amusing to our grubby minds. This was because the mask's rubber by our ears could vibrate rapidly from our expelled breathing in a vulgar "raspberry" sound. The same breath also quickly misted over the small window in the mask so we sat there as though in a fog. After a while the "all clear" would sound and we returned to our lessons. Occasionally the "all clear" was missed and we sat there longer than necessary until Mr. King, our teacher, thought enough was enough.

There was one incident at school that gave me more food for thought about the war. We were at play during our afternoon break when Mr. King came into the playground and calling for quiet, pointed out a large group of "our" aircraft flying in close formation high in the sky. There were dozens of them glinting silvery in the bright sunlight against a blue sky. It was a most impressive sight. During the next day or so, news came through that there had been a heavy daylight bomber raid either on Bristol, Cardiff or Swansea (I can't remember which). That news led me to realise the aircraft were not ours but a large escorted German bomber force. This led me to reflect upon how the enemy had the capability to fly in broad daylight over our country and clearly unmolested by any of our fighter planes. Even I as a child felt very vulnerable at the obvious weakness of our situation but I kept these thoughts to myself and if any other children thought the same they said nothing.

22 With Mum and Granny Moxey (Ada)

By standing at the back door of the farmhouse on autumnal and winter evenings in 1940, the signs of bombing raids on Bristol could be seen as we looked north across the moors and beyond the Mendip Hills. Bursts of anti-aircraft fire sparkled faintly in the black sky as did frequent flashes of bomb explosions. It made us feel lucky to be out of it but we had thoughts of those suffering there.

In September 1940, Mum paid a visit to me and stayed at the farmhouse. I now think that Dad had sent her to gain relief from the tensions of the heavy bombing at the time on London. Having travelled alone by train and bus she was exhausted when she arrived and not only from the journey. She was given some refreshments at the kitchen table and in just a few minutes had fallen fast asleep sitting on the long settle. Not understanding her weariness I said to Mrs. Stevens in surprise, "My mum's fallen asleep!" Raising a finger to her lips, Mrs. Stevens bade me to be quiet and to let her be. Childlike, it took me a few minutes to understand why Mum was not chatting to me about home and family and taking a walk with me around the orchard.

23 Me with my mum

24 In the orchard with Mum

25 At Glastonbury Abbey, 1940

At Shapwick School our geography lessons also included the progress of the war and to assist in this we were told to bring to school the newspapers that were no longer needed by the folks with whom we were billeted. So I had a regular supply of copies of the "Daily Mail" and for most of the days of each week it contained maps of battlefields in North Africa and the Russian front, as did other newspapers. These maps displayed large black arrows indicating the thrusts of the German armies in both areas. Everything seemed to be going very well for the Germans as they were pushing forward relentlessly, particularly on the Russian front. The class became proficient in the naming of those North African cities, ports and villages depicted as well as the names of a whole host of Russian cities. At that time the British government looked on the Russians as valuable allies having regarded them as enemies in the earlier years of the war.

The war in the North African desert then began to swing to-and-fro. At first it went well for our 8th Army who were sending the Italians into headlong retreat and thousands of their troops were surrendering. The apparent eagerness of these soldiers to give in became a joke among the British people. Any Italian, civilians and all, then became the butt of jokes in newspapers and popular songs.

Then the Italians were reinforced by German troops and our soldiers were being driven back. This back and forth continued for a long time until the Germans were finally driven to defeat starting with the battle of El Alamein. That was the start of good news about the war for us as all other news until then was worryingly bad. Similarly, an Italian army had earlier invaded Greece but was soon being taught a harsh lesson by the Greek soldiers. The Italians there and their leader Mussolini ("Il Duce") were also derided including by a popular song that started-

"Oh, what a surprise for the Duce, they do say they've had no spaghetti for weeks,

Oh, what a surprise for the Duce, they do say they can't put it over the Greeks"

and continued in the same vein for several verses. This kind of derision cheered us up for a while but then German reinforcements arrived and the Greek army was defeated.

One thing that cheered us up was a comedy show staged at Ashcott village hall for which Norman, Frank and I painted the posters. This was a fund-raising affair for comforts for the troops. The hall was packed with the evening's highlight being a comedian who had an enormous mouth with which he performed stunts by packing it with Ping-Pong balls and other unlikely objects. His jokes were received with delight with many against the Germans. The one I recall was about extravagant claims by the Nazis about their Luftwaffe attacks on us. Adopting a German accent the comedian said, "Last night our vunderful airmen flew a five hundred bomber attack on der Englanders. Later, five hundred and fifty of our planes returned". Not very funny now perhaps but we boys thought that it was terrific and repeated it for days.

As the manufacture of armaments gathered pace we began to see more of our aircraft flying over the Somerset countryside. These were mainly Spitfires, Hurricanes, Blenheim bombers and Westland Lysanders, the latter light aircraft being used for flying and bombing practice. We became quite competent at aircraft recognition but the most exciting to see were the two sorts of fighter aircraft mentioned above when they occasionally swept low in tight formation close over our heads and local fields. The Westland Lysanders were used to practice-bomb a target on the moors two or three miles from the village. The target was merely a plank triangle approximately seven yards long on each side, set on posts about waist high and painted white. It also had a flimsy structure within. About eight of we boys discovered it during one of our explorations over the fields and woods so went to have a closer look. Part of the timber had received a direct hit and had collapsed but we were fascinated to see splinters of aluminium bomb casings littered around it where small bombs had burst. Then in the grass we noticed a number of round holes about three inches diameter where other bombs had entered the peat. Stupid though it was, we thrust our hands down these in attempts to pull out a bomb as a souvenir but thankfully, we were never successful at this.

One outstanding event happened when five of us lads were playing football on a field at the village edge. About six loud explosions suddenly interrupted our game. Looking in the direction of the sound we saw several plumes of black smoke rising from the edge of the moor about two miles away. At almost the same time we saw an aircraft climbing steeply above the smoke to then level out high in the sky. Then three tiny figures, the aircraft's crew, fell from it to quickly be supported by parachutes to float gently to earth. After a short level flight the plane went into a steep dive to crash near Burtle. Of course our game was abandoned and assuming it was the enemy (as it turned out to be), we cheered going into a delirium of wild joy, laughing and rolling on the grass in sheer delight. Rising we linked arms across each other's shoulders to form a circle and indulged in a wild spinning dance.

We then rushed home to tea to tell excitedly of what we had seen. Norman bolted his food to then ride his bicycle swiftly away to the scene with me, bicycle less, watching his departure with envy. Later that evening he returned with a few souvenirs in the form of scraps from the smashed German plane. He also told of hearing about the German crew being surrounded by local people and surrendering except for one. He drew a pistol to threaten the watching crowd to keep them at bay. The story continued with the news that a local man had crept up behind the armed airman and knocked him out with a shovel. This was wonderful news and was the talk among we boys for weeks. The bombs may have been aimed in desperation at the single-track local railway but had fallen harmlessly. I can only suppose that the reason for the crash was that the aircraft had almost run out of fuel, as there was no explosion when it hit the ground.

Women called up for wartime service included those drafted into the land army sent to live on farms to help in food production. There was only one at Shapwick working at Manor Farm. Surprisingly, she had a young brother evacuee with us other Londoners in the village but living in a billet away from hers, an unusually convenient wartime arrangement of family contact with a younger sibling. She was not a pretty woman but her female attributes were obvious to the eye as she stood in her summer uniform of shirt, breeches and boots causing a frisson of desire in many a local male's mind. They expressed their view with the term, "That land girl working for Burough's be a voine looking woman".

Shapwick House, a grand Elizabethan mansion in the village, was reputedly haunted. There were stories sometimes mentioned by villagers about curious sounds being heard there and ghostly soldiers seen at night. It seems that some children who happened to be staying in the house overnight but in a room separate from their parents, had asked their parents, "Why were soldiers in my room last night?" When asked to describe them, they answered that they wore helmets and carried swords and other old fashioned weapons. It was concluded that they were images of Cromwell's troops that had been operating in the area at the time of the civil war. A variation of these sightings was of children seeing cowled monks in their room. All of the children, who reported these sighting were of infant years, say four or five. In 1941 this mansion was requisitioned as a convalescent home for our troops. Suddenly there were many young men strangers dressed in hospital blue walking about the village and the country lanes. They were the ones who were well on the way to recovery from what we boys imagined were battle wounds, but later it emerged that most had been suffering the usual injuries and illnesses to which we are all prone. A few of these soldiers took an interest in the unmarried village girls, thus providing unwelcome competition for the local bachelors. One socially responsible soldier even formed a scout group (un-uniformed) for all boys in the village. This group lasted for about the length of the summer holiday that year until the soldier was transferred.

26 Shapwick House

This use of the mansion gave some benefits for villagers in the form of live entertainment from ENSA (the forces Entertainments National Service Association). The actors and comedians were organised from among theatrical and other stage personalities called up for war service. Events provided for the soldiers were sometimes made available to civilians and so we attended two or three separate shows all of which we thoroughly enjoyed. A small admission charge was made that went towards some comforts for those convalescing. One soldier was a conjuror and magician who later gave a performance for the pupils in our class at the temporary school in the village hall. He was very entertaining and during his performance asked me to come forward to assist. He produced an egg from behind my ear and some other tricks of a similar nature before asking me to help him with a special bit of magic. Getting me to stand with one arm out from my side and the other crooked with my elbow down, he brought a gimlet and a tumbler from his table. Pretending to bore a hole in my elbow and muttering that I should pull a pained face he held the tumbler just below my elbow and then worked my other arm up and down like a pump handle. Magically, milk flowed into the glass and when full he drank it. The whole class erupted in applause at this as his grand finale and on sending me back to my desk he quietly said, "Rub your elbow as though it hurts", which it didn't of course and so I did. Later after school I was amazed to be asked by some of the more gullible children whether it hurt very much when he took milk from my arm!

In 1942/3 there were two separate arrivals of troops in lorries and Bren Gun carriers, the latter being open-topped armoured track-laying vehicles. They were parked in the village centre and the soldiers allowed us to clamber over them and told us how they worked. This was another excitement for boys. One of the carriers had within its open area a number of small gouges in the armour plating. We asked what they were and the driver said they were bullet marks. He added wistfully that one of his mates had been killed there when a German plane had strafed the vehicle. That made us think! The second arrival of troops was similar to the first but they stayed for a few days under canvas on a field near the mansion. Once again we were allowed to visit and see the equipment. When they left they did an exercise on an outlying field by circling its perimeter under the overhang of trees. This was practice to conceal their tracks from supposed patrolling enemy aircraft but as there were about forty vehicles a terrible mess was made of the farmer's pasture.

The other form of defence that we had was the Home Guard commanded by two retired army officers, Major Royle from the village and another major who lived on the far side of Shapwick Hill. The latter was quite deaf and when his men were asked a question by him they had to bellow an answer. Both were World War One veterans. Near the top of the hill was a newly built radio station with several tall masts being part of the nation's defence network. The duty of protecting this each night fell to the local Home Guard formed from farmers, including Mr. Stevens, their workmen, other men not called for war service and active pensioners. By the operation of a rota, these men protected this essential installation each night against the threat of enemy parachutists. It was said that because of a shortage of ammunition, the men were only issued with two 3.03 rounds each when on duty. In a macabre joke the men said that they were only given two because if they missed the enemy with the first shot they could shoot themselves with the second. The four man patrols occupied a small hut next to the station where two of the shift could get some sleep until they relieved their colleagues. The same men did not attend every night but a few times each month. These nightly patrols were there in all weathers and seasons. There was only one occasion when an alert was raised by one of a patrol who rushed into the shed to bellow at the deaf major the words, "Thar be zumone about zur". This shouting roused the resting men and all were ordered to fix bayonets and follow the major. Into the night they went cautiously, advancing together in the direction of the first sound. "Challenge him", commanded the major and one man shouted, "Who goes there?" There was no reply but a sound came from a different spot. Turning to it, the patrol crept closer when out of the gloom appeared a white horse! It was fortunate not to have been shot and had it been, its owner would have had something to say about it. The contemplation of this possibility caused some amusement in the village.

27 Operation 'Pied-Piper' saw the exodus of 1.9 million children from London

29 THRESHING

One winter morning at school there were curious sounds coming from the road fronting the school causing the pupils to stop working on their exercise books. The clanking, wheezing and rumbling became too much to bear without seeing its source. We started to climb onto our desk seats to see over the high sill of the school's main windows but were ordered to remain seated. After a moment's hesitation, we ignored the order and stood to see a steam-driven traction engine lumbering by, streaming black smoke and hauling a large salmon-pink box-like trailer. Unlike the local children we evacuees had never seen these machines before and were intrigued at the sight. When they had passed from view we resumed out seats and amazingly, had no rebuke from the teacher because of our disobedience. Perhaps she understood that our all-consuming curiosity had to be satisfied and that no harm was done. Our village friends soon told us that the pink box was a threshing machine worked by the engine that was to be used on various farms to thresh the sheaves stored in stacks and Dutch barns. We hoped to get involved with this activity and when we did, it proved to be one of the best events in the farming calendar.

The next time I saw this machinery was when it stood in Farmer Tucker's yard by Back Lane with the thresher set between two mows (stacks). The engine stood in line with them, about fifteen yards away and down-wind from the mows. I suppose that the wind direction was important because being coal fired, sparks from the engine's chimney could set the stacks ablaze if blown onto them. Both machines were linked by a continuous belt running from the large drive wheel on the engine to a smaller one protruding from the side of the thresher. The engine was always fired up when I saw it, sometimes driving the thresher, at other times it just stood idly, quietly wheezing to itself with a few moving parts lazily sliding back and forth. When fresh coal was fed to the boiler the chimney issued clouds of black smoke but in a while, a shimmering heat haze above the chimney top replaced this. It was the largest engine used on the village farms. Appearing clumsy and ungainly, it emanated an aura of tremendous and impressive power, seemingly a living thing. It was also very thirsty and like a farm animal, it had to be taken to a pond to drink. There, a large flexible reinforced hose with an end filter was lowered from the engine into the water through which it was pumped by the engine into its water tank, the engine sighing and wheezing as it did so.

Threshing a mow of wheat, oats or barley was a busy dusty job involving several men and a few boys. Men gradually dismantled it by throwing sheaves from the mow top to another man kneeling on top of the thresher. As the sheaves arrived their strings were cut and the wheat straw stems, including weed stalks, were roughly separated and fed into the machine through a wide slot before the kneeling man. The thresher had great versatility. Not only did it separate the grain from the ears and straw, it graded the grain into about three sizes sending these to outlets and into separate sacks. Weed seeds were also separated and fed similarly into another sack. Hooks kept the mouths of each sack open to receive the grain, The thresher could also sort straight, unbroken straws into sheaves for thatching, discharge broken straw for re-stacking for use as cattle bedding as well as chaff from the grain onto a heap on the ground. As it did all this, in the dusty air were clouds of thistledown as seed heads and stalks from this weed went through the machine. Boys kept watch on the sacks as they filled, ready to warn a man that they were almost full. When full he closed the outlet and opened an adjacent one diverting the same quality grains into an empty sack. He then removed the full sack replacing it with an empty one to await the procedure to be repeated. The other job for boys was clearing the heap of chaff by scooping it into large sacks.

Absorbing though this work was to us boys, the real fun for onlookers and us began when the stack was reduced to around one third of its original height. From there to the ground, nests of rats and mice were often found. They were comfortable homes for these vermin with an abundant food supply at hand. Boys stood around the reducing stack ready with sticks and accompanied by a dog or two, all waiting for the vermin to run. Though we had sticks to throw at rats I never saw one caught that way. Small gauge chicken-wire mesh was sometimes set up at the perimeter of the working area making escape by rats virtually impossible. The dogs knew when a rat was about to appear and their excitement mounted as the sheaves were removed one by one by the worker feeding them up onto the thresher. A dog might sometimes get almost under the feet of the man on the stack, ears pricked and concentrating in its eagerness to pounce on a rat it could smell. As a rat was exposed it sometimes leapt into the air to land several feet away in a rush for safety. Others might be caught in mid-air by a dog and shaken to death. Some rats might run a few yards twisting and turning this way and that but very few escaped. Dogs of the terrier type were particularly adept at ratting and could kill two in a moment if they emerged together. Mice being smaller had a better chance as they could more easily re-enter the stack lower down but the terriers usually caught them later.

The engine and threshing machine remained in the village for some weeks, engaged at the various farms. Then it would be gone, not to be seen until the next winter. Though we enjoyed these threshings it was hard work for the men but even they gained some amusement from our antics as we chased about.

30 ROAMING

Local boys and evacuees often roamed the fields together but usually it was a group of boys from London. I think it was because the local boys knew the parish well, whereas we found it new and adventurous. One favourite place was Loxley Wood a wonderful mature stand of oak trees where we spent hours engrossed in our fantasies of Robin Hood. Our making of bows and arrows from an abundance of hazel bushes that formed the under-storey of the trees helped these imaginings. In fact we were armed to the teeth at times with this assortment of stone axes, staves, slingshots and boluses. We even tipped our arrows with stone heads though not of flint but slate. We also made dens among the trees and bushes and lit campfires. The wood contained a line of stones each set about eight to nine yards apart and known as Swain's Jumps. They marked the exploits of a legendary local man. The story was that he had been captured by the King's soldiers during the Monmouth Rebellion and was being taken to prison or worse. The soldiers were camping overnight in the woods but before settling down to rest they engaged in some sport and trials of strength. Swain, on seeing their efforts at performing a series of long jumps said that he could do better. The soldiers scoffed at this but he insisted it was true. They gave him an opportunity to prove it and released his bonds. Going to his mark he produced a series of amazing bounds only to rush off to freedom before his captors could stop him. If the stone markers were a true record of this, he would have been an Olympic Champion in a later age.

28 Norman, me and Frank in front of a fallen walnut tree limb (orchard)

At other times we roamed the fields on explorations always making sure that we did not damage crops and that any gates that we went through were shut behind us. Even when walking across open fields, warlike thoughts were never far away. Walking in a bunch chatting amongst ourselves when for no reason at all, someone would shout, "Charge", and waving imaginary swords we rushed forward against an unseen enemy until out of breath, laughing we were forced to stop. At other times we played in or near the village often climbing the magnificent and tall elm trees that fringed several of the lanes sometimes reaching twenty-five yards or more until there were no more handholds or our nerves failed us. I discovered that it was easier to climb up some trees than climb down for as I descended a great elm, my extended handhold did not allow me to reach a foothold below. I was in a quandary of what to do and spent several minutes and getting in a panic about the trouble that I would be in if an adult had to bring a ladder to get me down. I then took a chance and embracing the broad trunk, I slid down it to catch a branch as it passed and I was safe. Another time I think that I nearly broke my neck. We were forbidden to climb onto the tops of hayricks or straw mows and with only very few exceptions we complied. There was one large stack of straw in one field that had been partly dismantled by the farmer so we thought we could not damage it if we climbed it as the thatch had been removed. When we reached the top we were about seven to eight feet high. I saw a deep heap of straw below that was very inviting as a landing place so I jumped. As I landed I found in an instant that it had been packed down by heavy rain and was only just soft enough to cushion my arrival. Even so, I was winded and felt a strain at the nape of my neck. Calling out to my mate Bob, who also was about to leap, I warned him not to come. We had often jumped into heaps of dry hay or straw in barns but my experience taught me a lesson to test each landing place first.

One of our long walks was to Moorlinch on the edge of Sedgemoor and on the far side of Shapwick Hill. Moorlinch Hill, a steep somewhat conical mound, was set off from the Polden Hills and was our objective that day. We climbed to the top to gaze at the view across the moor and then larked about on its thinly wooded slopes. As we walked down someone shouted, "Charge!" and as was our habit, we rushed down but not so fast as to become out of control. That is with the exception of Brian Turnbull. As we slowed he passed us with giant strides at which we all burst out laughing. Just before he hit a hedge that traversed the hill his cap flew off high in the air and that amused us further. Then he lowered his head and crashed horizontally into the hedge among the twigs and thorns, about a yard up. This was too much for us and we were helpless with mirth. Brian wasn't laughing though; instead he was in tears and stuck fast. Seeing his predicament we began to carefully extract him pushing aside twigs and branches as we lifted him clear with him rebuking us for our amusement at his expense. He had suffered scratches to his face and limbs with some bruises. He sobbed for a while afterwards as he was obviously shocked and hurt by what had occurred. A short while later we had to control ourselves a little more as he developed a fat, swollen lip. I suppose it wasn't very kind of us to be so amused by this but it was funny at the time and even after the passage of many years the memory of it still causes me to chuckle.

This episode decided us to return home but on the way we discovered a fresh burrow. By lying on the ground and listening at its entrance we heard snuffling within. Reaching into the burrow nothing could be felt so we tried smoking out whatever was there. Gathering dried grass we lit it at the mouth of the burrow and fanned the smoke into it. A further reaching and feeling we eventually touched something and as it was pulled free we saw that it was a large hedgehog curled in a spiky ball. It was decided to take it home as a trophy but being spiky, how could we carry it? One boy produced a handkerchief knotted into a sling and the animal was put inside. So we carried it the two to three miles back to our village only to let it go when we arrived. Within a few days Brian's swollen lip and scratches healed and then he too could see the funny side of things.

On one roaming, a West Ham boy boasted that he could eat stinging nettles. Disbelieving him we demanded that he demonstrate. Carefully picking about six of the tender tops, he crushed and rolled them with his hands into a dense ball. He then popped it into his mouth, munched for a few minutes and then swallowed. We were amazed not least, as he showed not a sign of discomfort. Though impressed, none among us followed his example.

We spent a lot of time within the village proper visiting various places of interest such as the blacksmith's forge, Tucker's rickyard at New Farm etc. At the latter a ram lived alone by a collapsed straw mow. This sheep had been raised by hand from a lamb and was very friendly in its own way to humans having the idea that it was fun to come behind someone and give a butt on the behind. This frightened us at first and though we were never fully at ease with it, we spent time being chased around the yard and over the large heap of straw. He was quicker than us and easily caught us up in a chase to give us a butt that was more of a nudge. This sent us tumbling down the heap in turn, laughing as he then chased another boy. It was not a game that we played for long because, as I have said, we did not fully trust him. Farmer Tucker sometimes used a lean-to barn at one end of this yard for milking. He employed boy on this and other simple tasks on his farm. Sadly, the boy was simple and was seldom seen about the village on his own. We never took advantage of him on those rare occasions when we found him alone though we were amused to see him at times as he sat on his stool milking whilst dissolving into fits of giggles for no apparent reason. Poor lad!

Though a few farmers kept flocks of sheep they mostly concentrated on dairy. Some landless villagers also kept a few and rented small fields for their grazing. One day we came across two men in a barn shearing a ram and a ewe. They were using old-fashioned shearing clippers (not powered of course) and each man held an animal between his legs as he removed the fleece, the sheep helpless as they half lay with legs uppermost. It was interesting to watch and as one man sheared the lower abdomen of the ram he took hold of a large woolly bag suspended there and said to me, "How'd you like a pair like these young'un?" That made us boys giggle.

Beerways Farm, where we sometimes played with the farmer's younger sons, also had a flock and was the scene of a surprise for me. It was springtime and strolling back home to lunch after our play, though we passed quietly through the flock, we startled a ewe that ran a little way ahead. She suddenly half squatted with hind legs spread and in an instant and a rush a lamb was born. Having heard stories of some cows having suffering a long labour when calving the sight was astonishing. Returning after our meal, we saw that the ewe was now mothering two more lambs so birthing was easy for her. We once came upon a dead sheep and as we looked we saw that crows had pecked its eyes out. Gruesome, but the nature of things I suppose.

We also roamed about the private grounds of Shapwick House but never dared enter its forecourt close to the mansion frontage but kept beyond the ha-ha wall. There was an interesting wood in part of the grounds containing an old stone-built dovecote with a lantern at its top allowing access for birds to the interior. In its heyday this building would have provided plump pigeon fledglings for many pies for the benefit of the gentry. The entrance door to the dovecote was never locked so we had easy access. Within, it had very many nesting holes in tiers lining the perimeter wall with yet more in a central column. The pigeons had long been ousted by an invasion of jackdaws that then used it to rear their own young. We used the pigeonholes to climb to the topmost tiers in a quest for eggs or the pleasure of seeing nestlings but we always timed our visits too late.

Our invasion of these grounds must have been a slight shock for the owners and I doubt if any village children had been as bold before. One day when playing near the edge of the wood close to the entrance drive I glanced aside to see an elderly lady glowering at us through the foliage. She was elegantly dressed in an old-fashioned gown and three-quarter-length coat with a wide-brimmed hat on her head. From her severe expression I knew she was not pleased by our presence. With a yell of, "Look out!" I dashed away followed closely by my mates but nothing more was said and we continued to visit at will afterwards. Also in the grounds was a moat that once surrounded an ancient dwelling long since gone. Eels abounded in the moat and when the water was low they were seen basking on the mud in the shallows. Provided that one was prepared to wade in the mud they were easily caught in a bucket.

Nearby was a large rookery where some villagers with shotguns came in spring to bag fledgling rooks. The young birds were at an early stage of learning to fly and so were easy targets as they sat on or hopped among branches in the treetops. Only a proportion was shot to be taken home to be made into rook pies. I had this dish once, as it was a speciality of Granny Moxey. Having enjoyed my meal Mrs. Stevens asked if I knew what it was I had eaten. I replied it was chicken pie. When told what it was I could not believe my ears and it was further remarked to me if I had known I probably would have refused it. That was true I suspect but I can recommend the pie now.

During some of my meanderings in the village I found myself in trouble from being inadvertently impudent. Mr. Williams who was the blacksmith at Ashcott was a strong, powerfully built pleasant man. He occasionally came to Shapwick where his nickname among the adult male villagers was "Banger", obviously a little joke that I was unaware of about his hammering of iron. I heard this nickname mentioned and thought that he knew of it and accepted it. I was sitting on the orchard gate with my pal Bob when Mr. Williams came cycling by with another man. "Hello Banger", I said in a friendly way. Braking, he dismounted and wheeled his machine to me. Pointing threateningly at me he said, "If thee call I that agin, young-un, I'll clip thy yur (ear)". I was mortified, for a clip around the ear by him would have knocked my head off into the middle of next week. Unsurprisingly, I never addressed him that way again.

Another incident concerned a teenage youth and a health drink advertised at the time called "Kruchen's Salts". Again, I heard the nickname "Kruchens" applied to the youth, which I also thought that he had accepted. Walking along Kent Lane, Bob and I met the youth and another lounging on a gate. "Hello Kruchens", said I at which the youth called me a cheeky young bugger and lunged at me giving a heavy slap to my cheek. Again, that was the last time I called him by that name. The lesson I gained about nicknames was to take care to whom they were applied, but it took a second incident for it to sink into my brain. I later understood what "Kruchen's" was all about when I saw the product and its label. It included a comic cartoon of a red-faced man with a large chin and bright eyes under raised eyebrows, supposedly portraying health and vigour for the middle-aged and elderly. The cartoon bore a striking resemblance to the offended youth.

We also explored the few local quarries in outlying fields, one with an abundance of fossils but unfortunately all of the same type of a small common seashell. However, we became enthusiastic collectors of fossils when our teacher Mr. King, told us that as part of his lesson about prehistoric times and its creatures, he was offering a fifteen shillings (seventy-five new pence) National Savings Certificate to the pupil with the best collection. Of course everyone had a collection of those I have described but to find others that were different was impossible or so it seemed. Then I remembered a stone that lay in a pasture that we had often idly examined and cast aside. The stone was about half the size of a house brick and had a small imprint of an ammonite so I made sure to get it. On closer examination it bore some tiny imprints and raised fossil areas on other surfaces. It clinched the prize for me and I felt rich.

Sundays were to my friends and me the dullest days of each week as we were required to dress in our best clothes, behave ourselves, not to be noisy and keep our clothes and selves clean. So roaming was curtailed. When the weather was dry on these days we loitered at the village crossroads talking and indulging in banter but on wet Sundays it was worse as we were confined indoors escaping only to church or Sunday School neither of which was very liberating. On fine Sunday afternoons members of individual families went for a walk together which was a relief from the solemnity of the day and gave opportunity for farmers to see how crops on other farms were progressing. Worst of all were summer weekdays and weekends when we boys were confined to house during a long spell of rain. Sometimes it seemed it rained non-stop for a fortnight and apart from attending school we felt imprisoned and restless. It was also difficult to be allowed out to feed our pet rabbits. I once had to pretend to visit the outside toilet only to scamper to the barns to thrust a manglewurzle into to their hutch. The rabbits there were half starved and had eaten every scrap of their bedding to quell their hunger. A very sad state of affairs!

Snowfall was a different matter and on Saturdays and during holidays we were allowed to roam when it stopped. This gave rein to all of the usual snowball fights and the rolling of giant snowballs. At the start of 1942 there was a particularly heavy fall that became wind-blown to form small drifts and filled boundary ditches. This gave opportunity to slice with our hands large blocks of snow from them to throw at each other. That was the best snow-fight fun ever. Sliding on "Greasy Pond" was also a favourite sport and after the first two or three hard frosts we then tentatively tested the strength of the ice to see if it would bear our weight. One boy would volunteer to walk the ice but that sometimes brought ominous sounds of cracking like distant rifle fire causing him to get off the ice without delay. When the ice was strong we had hours of fun on its surface but it was not without hazard. I once pitched forward onto my face and thumped my nose hard causing it to bleed profusely. Sobbing and bawling I ran home but as it was a Sunday and boisterous play was forbidden I spoke a half-truth by explaining that I had slipped over. What all of this sliding did to our boots I hardly like to think of now but I suppose it increased the need of repairs considerably.

One thing that the village children showed us to do was how to make whistles from live sycamore twigs. By cutting off a young woody shoot about the thickness and length of a pencil the leaves were stripped off. Then the bark at its mid-point was cut through to the wood around its circumference. One end of the bark was tapped repeatedly with a penknife handle to gently bruise it until it could be slipped off as a tube. Before doing so, a notch was cut into the bark and wood beneath. When the bark was off a sliver of wood was cut from the notch to the mouthpiece. Replacing the bark with the notches coinciding the surplus end of the stick was cut away and the whistle could be blown. These worked until the bark dried but I suspect that this little craft is rarely practiced now.

31 VILLAGE ELEMENTARY EDUCATION

29 Me - Ted Baverstock with my evacuated class – second row down, third from left with white collar dark tie and dark jacket.

Though I went to three schools among two villages my recollection of my time at the first, Ashcott Elementary School, is very hazy as my attendance there lasted only a few weeks before I moved to Shapwick. What remains in my memory of Ashcott School is that except for its environs, there was little difference between life there and the one I had known at Dawson School in Dagenham. I suppose that this was because I was with a fairly large number of pupils from my former school together with two or three of our original teachers. Moreover, we attended full-time. When Frank and I arrived at Shapwick Elementary School there were relatively few evacuees there and the premises were smaller; comprising one large and one small classroom with cloakrooms and outside lavatories. The village children and evacuees could not all be accommodated at the school together so for the first several weeks they attended mornings and we afternoons. I suppose extra desks were obtained and then all evacuees were accommodated together in the smaller of the two classrooms previously used by the local infants and we then attended full-time. Mr. King, a decent man and a good teacher at Dagenham, taught us at Shapwick. He had our interests at heart but that isn't to say that he wasn't strict but not excessively so. It must have been difficult for the established village teachers and also he, as each classroom had a range of age groups from five to fourteen in the main room and from seven to almost fourteen in the smaller.

Soon after our arrival at Old Farm, Frank and I were invited by Mr. King to have tea with his family and himself in the schoolhouse. We accepted this singular offer and when telling Mrs. Stevens the news, she gave us a curious glance. We subsequently attended and had a pleasant time in their company and then returned to the farm thinking no more of it. It was months later that I realised that there was a meaning behind this as no other boys had such an invitation. I thought that he and his wife (née Thompson a former teacher at Campbell Senior School where my sisters attended) wished to reassure themselves that we were being properly fed. It is true to say that both Frank and I were small for our years, thin of build and pale-faced. Anyway, both adults seemed satisfied about our welfare and nothing more was said but it does explain the look that Mrs. Stevens shot at us.

As an adult I have come to realise that at the schools that I attended, boys (or perhaps I should say urchins) were not only in a survival of the fittest situation but in some ways also rather like junior tribal savages. Our arrival in Shapwick must have come as a shock to the village boys who in the main were more civilized and quieter. At my former Dagenham school there was a similar contest to decide where individuals stood in the pecking order among one's classmates and friends and that state of affairs probably still persists at some if not all, present day schools. It certainly was the case with our arrival at Shapwick but with greater emphasis as it had a small pupil roll compared to the two to three hundred at Dagenham's Dawson School. The fifty or so pupils at Shapwick were under constant scrutiny for weaknesses at least by the older boys. I already knew some Dagenham boys now at Shapwick but among them were a few strangers who had been accompanied by older or younger siblings. The oldest and biggest at thirteen was Harry Stoddart who was the informal leader of our group and with whom I did not get along. He gave the lead to many other boys in jeering at me and generally making my life uncomfortable. I can only suppose that this was because I was small for my age and was relatively well dressed, a principle that my parents were at pains to achieve. Being tidily dressed was taken by the boys as a sign of pampering by parents, which I don't think I was. This marked me out as a sissy, a state of affairs that continued on and off for the first few weeks in the minds of Harry and his pals. This all changed one day.

Mr. King said that he was going to arrange a boxing match one evening for the class. All boys over nine years would take part. I got my parents to send the two pairs of boxing gloves I had at home and other sets were provided from elsewhere. When we arrived at our classroom on the appointed evening we found that desks had been arranged in a square with their fronts facing inwards. We were told to sit on the tops of these with our legs hanging within the square, thus making a boxing ring minus ropes but with a relatively soft flesh and bone boundary for the boxers within. Mr. King then chose categories of contestants on the basis of size and age being roughly 9 - 10, 11 - 12, and 12 - 13 age groups. So the battles began comprising three rounds for each match involving a series of around three different sets of opponents in each category; the youngest group starting the evening off with Mr. King as referee and timekeeper for all bouts. Each pair of opponents set about each other with gusto, arms flailing and fists flying. First one boxer and then the other was forced back against the surrounding knees of classmates who leaned back out of harm's way. As the action took place there were shouts of encouragement and cheers from the audience. No one got badly hurt though there were a few nosebleeds and the whole evening was one of excitement and afterwards deemed a great success by most if not all.

The next day when in the playground, to my surprise I found that Harry Stoddart was behaving in a friendly and chatting manner towards me as were his gang of older boys. It dawned on me that this sudden change was because I must have performed well enough the night before and my status had been transformed. I was converted from sissy to fighter and excepting for one boy and a few others on rare occasions, I was seldom troubled by aggression thereafter. The final accolade came a few evenings later when I was with Norman and Frank watching Jim Brewer milking Old Farm's cows in the cow stall when the boxing match was mentioned by Jim. He was a local youth aged about seventeen who was occasionally employed to help with milking. He remarked upon what he had heard about the boxing and said, "Which one of you young-uns is Ted?" Frank said, "He is", pointing at me. Jim then regarded me with a slight look of admiration for a moment. In my childish way I thought that I was famous; well at least in the village. I still had to take care not to rile the bigger boys but I found that if I could make them laugh I could get away with a few liberties. In fact I became the recognised joker among my pals and though I did not realise it at the time, it acted as a defence mechanism helping to deflect aggression. That evening of boxing held me in good stead for the four years I lived in the village because, as luck would have it, I advanced in the pecking order to the top as the older and bigger boys left.

This boxing event did not entirely settle things as fights still broke out on occasions. I found myself involved in a few and though fists were used at the start of a fight, it then developed into a wrestling bout as we hugged each other and tried throwing each other down. Inevitably, this ended with both rolling on the playground surface in a rough embrace, panting and puffing. During one of these situations I heard my opponent breathing heavily and had the idea of squeezing his chest hard when he exhaled. By gripping very tight it had the effect of almost stopping his breathing and as he gasped I demanded, "Give in?" After some further resistance he did and I had won. I used this technique at other times but it was no good with the bigger and stronger boys who had got the measure of my technique.

However, there was one boy, Albert, of about my own age, that I could not cope with. He was a bit slow-witted and to me, rather primitive and of a frighteningly tough, sinister appearance. I also had the impression that he had been badly treated at his home in London and that had hardened him. I sensed that in a serious confrontation he would not know when to stop when handing out a beating. His casual form of punishment was applying a torture by grinding his knuckles into his victim's temples as he grinned with malicious enjoyment. I can vouch how painful it was. My trouble was that William, a village boy and I were enemies and had some skirmishes that he always lost. Albert was his minder so William later reported these fights to him, leading to Albert coming looking for me to apply the torture. This then caused me later to whack William in revenge and the cycle of me being tortured and taking revenge went on and on. It was stupid of me but I kept at it because I hoped that William would eventually stop telling Albert. The cycle only stopped when Albert returned to London. Other fights that occurred rarely were between two girls. As spectators, we horrible boys enjoyed these most of all. They were known as "Cat fights", and involved scratching, biting, hair pulling and rolling on the ground. We gathered around the combatants cheering and encouraging them just as we did with boy fights.

As was normal in boy's schools there were various categories of punishment for misbehaviour or slackness. A boy invited punishment sometimes because he had not thought though the consequences of a mischievous action. One such activity of ours in class was to flick paper pellets, or even ink sodden ones, at each other by the use of a ruler. They had the advantage of being silent in use. One boy took things too far by bringing some maize seeds (poultry food) into class to use as missiles. Excellent though they were, when he shot the first one off it ricocheted around the room noisily. It caused the rest of the class to giggle and the boy to be invited to the front of the room for the cane. The mildest punishment meted out was one whack on the palm with the flat of a ruler, which though fairly painful it got the punishment over and done with. The next worse punishment was "lines" requiring one sentence such as "I must not talk or misbehave in class", to be written out one, two or three hundred times depending on the severity of the offence. If in a bad mood with a culprit, Mr. King would order three hundred lines and spontaneously compose a sentence running to three lines of writing. So the agony was made even more onerous and drawn out, giving the victim a feeling of despair. The only way of easing its impact was by editing it slightly so that a few words were dropped or the sense slightly modified so that completed sheets handed in were accepted without the teacher noticing, or so we thought. This punishment had to be done when all other pupils were enjoying their playtimes at mid-morning/afternoon breaks. The sound of their fun compounded the victim's unhappiness as he sat under the gaze of the teacher in the otherwise empty classroom.

The worst punishment of all was the cane. This was reserved for the most heinous of bad behaviour and was administered in any number of strokes up to a limit of six, either a single stroke on the palm of the hand; two strokes, one on each palm; or six strokes, three on each palm. These strokes stung very much but it was a point of honour among us not to cry though some boys returned to their desks with eyes brimming with tears after a caning. That was acceptable as long as there weren't any sobs. Though the cane hurt it was bearable and after the fear of an initial caning it became a badge of toughness among the boys but, again, only if there weren't tears and sobs. After a caning when we were later together in the playground, the victim was crowded around and asked to show his palms. This he did with some pride. The stroke marks each had a central white line with its margins in red. A feeling of numbness persisted in the hand(s) for an hour or more. I had all of these punishments at one time or another.

There was one more punishment that I should mention at this stage. I was called from my desk to that of Mr. King's to account for some poor work in an exercise book. Speaking sharply to me as he read the text he suddenly rapped me on the side of my jaw with his knuckles. I immediately felt myself swaying slightly as my senses reeled and vision began to blur. However, I managed to stay on my feet and in a trice I was my usual self. Mr. King looked at me intently for a moment and then brusquely told me to return to my desk. Sitting down I knew that he had inadvertently delivered what was almost a knockout blow. I also knew that though he wished to give my face a swipe he did not mean to really harm me. He never hit any boy around the face again.

There was one famous occasion when almost all boys in the class got the cane. It was winter and there had been several hard frosts. This led to margins of streams being frozen and the surface ice on ponds becoming capable of bearing the weight of several boys sliding on its surface at once. That day I returned from my midday meal to the school with only a minute or so to spare to find the playground almost deserted. Those few of us there, were called into our class where most desks were empty. Mr. King demanded of us the whereabouts of the others but no one knew. After a moment or so in the ensuing silence, the sound of shouts and laughter could be heard from the direction of the village shop. I was told to go to find my classmates and to tell them to return to school immediately. Setting off and following the sounds I arrived at "Greasy Pond" near to the shop to discover all those who were missing having a wonderful time sliding on its frozen surface. In the din I had difficulty in telling them my message and it was clear they had lost all track of time. Before we returned, I couldn't miss the chance to have a few slides myself.

When we all trooped into the classroom, the latecomers were told to stand in line as Mr. King brandished his cane. In succession, they all received two strokes and many returned to their seats rubbing hands ruefully. However, there was one act of bravado that impressed us all. When Harry Stoddart stepped up for his caning and held out his hand, Len Wallace, his second in command, stepped forward and pushed Harry's hand away and put his there instead. This was courageous stuff and we were all full of admiration. Mr. King paused for a moment, then whacked the cane down hard and then hard on Len's other hand. This bravado had no effect as Harry got his share immediately following. Afterwards, I was made to feel by my mates that I should have been there with them and that their punishments were partly my fault. They soon got over it when I told them truthfully that I would have been on the pond with them if I had known. As with the ancient Greeks, it was a case of turning against the bearer of bad news.

For the first few weeks lessons continued in a routine with the few seven and eight year-olds being taught in the same classroom as the older boys as I have said, some almost fourteen years. Then there was a period when we were required to attend Ashcott village hall for joint singing lessons with other evacuees. We trooped the two miles there about once per month accompanied by our teacher. The senior teacher at Ashcott, Mr. Townley, was the one who last taught a previous class of mine at Dagenham and it was he who organised and conducted us in our songs. He was much stricter than Mr. King and was rather free with a hard smack on the face of an offending pupil, as I had earlier discovered. We sang a variety of songs as Townley stood on the stage and waved his arms about keeping us more or less in time as we sang with gusto.

Of all songs we were required to sing, "London's Burning" as a canon was sung the loudest. Considering the bombing and incendiary raids with which the Germans were threatening London and other British cities, it was a very insensitive choice by our conductor. News of the blitz on London often made us think of our families there, hoping that they were safe. Younger children and girls stood in the front rows of the hall and we other boys were towards the back. One day when we were bellowing this song, a lot of nudging took place among the boys. This nudging was accompanied with an indication to look up. Because of some peculiarity of the hall's acoustics, the lamp bowls hanging on long chains from the ceiling were swinging to-and-fro. We sensed that it was the sound of our voices so we tilted our heads back to direct the full force of our bellowing at them. This had the effect of causing them to swing more and more and then, wildly. We were overjoyed with the effect and were all grinning ear to ear. But Mr. Townley saw what was happening, stopped conducting and called to us to stop. We were so engrossed with our achievement as we stared upwards, it was several seconds before his shouts were heard and we came to a ragged stop. The lamps continued to swing but gradually subsided to a stop. We never sang "London's Burning" again.

Back at Shapwick School in a subsequent week, we were surprised to find that our class had an additional teacher who was there to deal with the younger boys. He also took over the control of the whole class in the absence of Mr. King. His name was also Mr. Townley, being the artist brother of the teacher at Ashcott but the contrast between the two was stark. Our Mr. Townley was slight in build, quietly spoken and of a gentle nature. A withered right arm also physically handicapped him. Sad to say, it was only a week or two before we children had the measure of him and started to make his life difficult but only when Mr. King was absent. On these occasions we chatted among ourselves, flicked pellets of paper at each other and also at the teacher. As we became ever more unruly he stood before us in dismay and our wicked triumph was complete. He did not deserve us and within a few more days he was gone and we never saw him again. This unruliness continued to a lesser extent with Mr. King who I think was trying to understand that absence from our homes may have been upsetting us and was making allowances. Though he was fairly strict he seemed to sense that he too was losing control of us. One day this caused him to send a boy to Mr. Townley at Ashcott to ask him to come to us. He duly arrived and gave us a stern talking to that calmed us down. We knew that he was a man who would brook no defiance and any sign of it would be severely dealt with.

30 Shapwick Village School

So life fell into a routine at the school and we continued to be taught in the same classroom with the same teacher. Games in the playground at break-time continued in the same way as they had in the streets at home. Football with a tennis ball was the most popular with us, the games ranging up and down the tarmacadam surface as we dodged with the ball on our pitch between girls and small children, themselves engaged in their own play. One game resulted in the ball being kicked high in the direction of the schoolhouse standing adjacent to the playground. With horror we watched it disappear, seemingly in slow motion, through a pane of glass in an upper window. Of course we said nothing but the next day an irate Mr. King, who lived there with his wife and infant son, demanded to know the culprits. We owned up and so nine of us were told that we would be paying for the repair. A week later we were told that the cost was one shilling and sixpence so that would be tuppence each, which we duly handed over. This curbed our football games at first but they were soon back being contested as vigorously as before but with no further accidents.

Many of our other games were on the rough and tumble side mostly in the form of remembered traditional London street games. We invented a few of our own, the one I most clearly recall we named "Whiplash". We hit on the idea of forming a long single file of boys holding hands, all running as fast as possible to our left and pulling the line along for about fifteen yards in one direction. Then the leader doubled the line outwards in a sharp U-turn back towards the start. As the file snaked around on itself, so centrifugal force sent the tail-enders racing along in a wide arc. The last two or three were careering round with "giant" strides until the centrifugal force strained their grip on each other till it was unbearable. Caused to let go they rushed along as separate individuals in a wild running motion trying to keep their footing but often ending up in a heap. This game became very popular despite the bruises and grazes we suffered. Then one of us thought of a variation and said, "Let's get some of the girls to be tail-enders", and so we coerced them into the line. We took it gently with them at first but could not resist giving them the full experience. They weren't interested in continuing after that. So we turned our attention to the smaller boys. Following the same approach as with the girls it wasn't long before they too were flying out of control along the playground. Finally, after one playtime break the teachers noticed that there were a number of their pupils coming back to the classroom looking rather battered. Their enquiries as to the cause led to the banning of "Whiplash" thereafter.

Some other practices that we inflicted on each other and innocents among us were "Chinese Burns" and scorching. With the former, a child was asked to present his bare forearm to a bigger boy who then gripped it with both hands to twisted the victim's skin in opposite directions. This was not done to excess but from my own experience the sensation it momentarily caused was remarkably like a burn. The latter practice involved the use of a magnifying glass on a sunny day and persuading a victim to present a bare forearm. The boy with the lens then said, "Look how bright the light is on your skin" before focussing the light beam into a tiny spot. The victim then gave a satisfying yelp as he snatched his arm away. These lenses came into use in another way. Black or red ants (Emmets) that got into our shirts sometimes stung us when we romped about on grass. So sprawled on the ground, we took revenge by chasing them with a focussed beam as they crawled about on paving stones. When caught they exploded with a gratifying pop.

Some games went in cycles of crazes arriving spontaneously and lasting for a few weeks only to stop just as suddenly. A prime example of this concerned the making of paper aeroplanes each from one page of an exercise book. On dry days when the air was at least fairly calm they could be successfully thrown to float in the air. During a craze these planes became thick in the air, some flying for several metres. Some other toys we made ourselves but these were mostly used outside school time and included bows and arrows, spears, stone axe/choppers, boluses and sling shots. One lad brought his slingshot to school un-noticed by teachers because they were easily concealed in a pocket away from adult eyes. The boy was an expert with it and having gathered a few stones the size of an infant's fist, he would whirl them one at a time on the sling's pad. Letting one of the two thongs of the sling loose, the stone was hurled from the playground over low trees and bushes opposite into Happy Harry's orchard to a distance of sixty to seventy- yards. It was of a slight resemblance to the technique of the biblical David. I cannot bear to think what the outcome would have been if one of these missiles had by chance struck Harry but they never did. I think that his chickens foraging in his orchard were at severe risk though.

In cold winter weather after frost and a shower of rain or snow, another traditional game of ice sliding automatically suggested itself. At first the slide on the playground gave poor results but by persistent sliding in the same place the slide became smooth, shiny, very slippery and about eight to ten yards long. Sliding warmed us up nicely during our break-time and excluded all other ideas of play. Just as with the "Whiplash" game, the younger children who attempted to slide fell, frequently returning to class bruised and limping. When this happened, Mr. King soon appeared with a bucket of ash from the stove to scatter it along the length of the slide. That stopped our fun.

On bitterly cold days we were allowed, if we so wished, to stay in the classroom to warm ourselves around the iron stove. It was a

"Tortoise Stove" standing at the teacher's end of the classroom. Its lid bore an embossed image of a tortoise and the words, "Slow but sure". As necessary during the day the fire was replenished with coke by one of the older boys putting it through a round-lidded hole on the top. As a safety precaution an iron railing surrounded it and in bitter weather about six or so of us leaned on this and chatted together. We discovered that if we dropped some spit on the hot lid, the spit jumped and jiggled around till it ended as a black, burnt-out speck. One cold day, "Jonesy", one of the younger boys had a brainwave and left us only to quickly return with a snowball, which he dropped onto the hot lid. There was an immediate hiss and splutter as the snow was rapidly converted to steam and boiling water as everyone recoiled from it. It also made a slightly sooty mess around the stove about which the teacher said nothing seemingly not noticing. Of course we said nothing but we told Jonesy how stupid he was. Later it was noticed that the cast iron lid had a slightly wavy crack in it from the centre to the edge resultant of the thermal shock between sudden freeze to near red heat. It was a constant reminder of Jonesy's mad escapade.

In these colder winter months the classrooms being inadequately heated caused children seated furthermost from the stoves to suffer from the cold. This was particularly so in the larger classroom that had a very high ceiling. It was noticeable during these cold times our teachers tended to do a lot of instruction from the close vicinity of a stove. For our part, in the most severe cold we sat at our desks well clothed in jerseys, jackets and sometimes overcoats, as well as scarves and caps. Discovering that our ears stayed cold we adopted a technique of wearing these scarves over our heads to cover them. With the scarf ends around our necks, the whole was held in place by our caps perched on top. This habit served us in good stead when roaming the village and fields in the cold. Another technique for outdoors involved "Winter Warmers". Finding an empty tin can, several holes were pierced in its sides with a short length of wire laced through opposite holes to provide a bucket-like handle. The tin was then stuffed with a mixture of hay and rags. A yard-long string was then tied to the wire and the hay/rag mix was set alight. When it took hold the can was whirled around by the string and with the draught this caused the fire grew bright and the tin red-hot. Thus we had our personal heaters. These devices also produced a satisfying stream of smoke when whirled about.

My evacuee companion Frank, was a person who possessed the most violent and uncontrollable temper that I ever saw in a child or even an adult. If riled by the slightest provocation, his face contorted with fury, his mouth dribbled and slightly foamed, he breathed in hisses, his hands took on a claw-like mode, and he bared his teeth to then rush headlong at his tormentor. Most boys at sometime in their school years had to suffer taunts of one sort of another and sometimes about their names. Frank's surname was Crann and from the acceptable nickname "Cranny" some began to call him "Cracks and Crannies" or even "Granny" a mild enough tease but Frank became beside himself with rage and blindly rushed at the boys taunting him. Of course, when the others saw his reaction they joined in and Frank became even more outraged and frantic. This state of affairs once happened on an afternoon in the school playground. In his fury, Frank took from his pocket a penknife and threw it at one of his teasers. At the time I noted that the knife was shut so Frank was not totally out of control. Perhaps in his hysteria, did he not think to open the blade or was it a warning of worse to come? This act came to the attention of Mr. King. When we were back at our desks, Mr. King confiscated Frank's knife.

Later that day I was indoors at the farm but Frank was unusually absent. After about forty-five minutes Mrs. Stevens became concerned and told me to search for him. I found him in the school having a barely restrained confrontation with Mr. King. In a slightly tremulous voice, Frank was demanding the return of his knife but Mr. King stood his ground and refused. Could he have done otherwise? Of course not! This situation had been going on since the end of the school day. An argument of this nature with a teacher was something quite unique in my experience. The teacher obviously surmised that Frank had a temper that he was barely controlling and was making some allowance for it. After a moment or two at this scene I intervened saying, "Come on Frank, come home. It's tea-time and Mrs. Stevens is worried about you". This did the trick and was, I suppose, a let-out for Frank who came home with me, still slightly seething but calming as we walked. A few days later the knife was returned but with a warning to Frank never to throw it again.

This incident reduced the teasing that Frank received from the other boys. Never the less, there were similar incidents between him,

Norman and myself at Old Farm. Two that stand out were as follows. We three were in the orchard and something caused Frank to go into a rage at Norman. His fury seemed excessive to us others but he came at Norman teeth bared, etc, and with claws outstretched aiming for Norman's face. Norman stood his ground white faced to merely clench his right fist and hold his arm rigidly before him shoulder high. Frank continued his blind charge and ran onto the fist that struck him full in the mouth. Frank recoiled to end flat on his back on the orchard grass howling. That finished the confrontation and calm gradually resumed as Frank's tears lessened. Another time when we were indoors, Frank had worked up into a level approaching a full temper when we others thought to calm him by tickling. Wrestling him to the floor, we tickled his armpits and his neck. Frank laughed quite heartily and then even more so. Norman and I thought that we had discovered the answer to Frank's outbursts and so stopped the tickling. Immediately, Frank's face darkened and the snarling, bared teeth rage resumed so he got tickled again. We stopped, Frank raged, we tickled, then stopped, Frank raged, and so on for a while. In the end we beat a retreat out of Frank's way until he calmed. I have to say that Frank seemed to be dangerous at these times but nothing very serious ever happened among us.

Life at school carried on with myself being reasonably good at my lessons except arithmetic with which I often struggled. When the blitz on London started in earnest in September 1940, it caused another wave of London evacuees aged from seven to thirteen, about twenty in all, to descend on Shapwick. They were from West Ham and were mostly boys but a few girls were with them, being siblings of some. One, Sid Witherington, was billeted at Old Farm as Frank had left to attend another school elsewhere in Somerset. This influx upset the pecking order among the boys not least because the West Ham boys were reputed to be tough. There was a showdown one Saturday between two twelve year old boys one from each group, our champion being Sid Stoddart. It started more or less under the rules for boxing with boxing gloves, both camps shouting encouragement to their respective schoolmates. The fight developed into a real battle and it became apparent that Sid was winning. At that the supporters of his West Ham opponent shouted, "Take off the gloves. Use bare fists", thinking it would give their boy an advantage but he suffered an even bigger beating and Sid won. That made the Dagenham boys feel much more confident in our dealings with them. They had with them their own aged schoolmaster, Mr. Berry, having been brought out of retirement. As there was insufficient room for his pupils at the school, the village hall was allocated to them as a schoolroom. So for the following several months they were educated there and we at the school proper.

31 Shapwick Village Hall

There were two visits paid to the school by outsiders causing nervous excitement among the children. One was the legendary "Nit Nurse" who took her station in the small classroom temporarily emptied of pupils where she rummaged through the hair of a succession of pupils. No one was ever found to be infested, or at least as far as I knew except for some subsequent instances. Unfortunately, these later results did not dispel the idea that was later common among some local village women that all evacuees had arrived from London flea infested. There were a few incidents of nits in one or two evacuees but these occurred many months after our arrival so had been picked up locally but this inevitably reinforced the rumour mentioned. The other school visitor was a travelling dentist who came to inspect and treat us with an array of equipment that he set up in the same classroom. His arrival caused a frisson of fear among all as lurid stories were exchanged, some warning how painful his treatment would be. To a greater or lesser extent, the warning proved to be true when we found that our mouths were probed with sharp instruments, gums spiked with hypodermic needles and teeth drilled. Using a foot pedal worked by an up and down motion the drill was operated by the dentist. Unlike the modern dentist's drills, the spin of his was rather slow and vibrated the tooth being excavated. If the cavity was deep, it became painful even after its area was anesthetized. Several of us re-emerged from the torture holding our jaws and looking distressed only to trouble fellow pupils with lurid and barely truthful reports with how terrible it was.

When parcels came from home, contents that I looked forward to most other than sweets were the few children's cartoon comics. At first these were the Beano, the Dandy and Film Fun but when I reached the age of eleven to twelve, I was introduced to others of a more adventurous content. They were the Adventure, Champion, Rover and Wizard and my friends and I absorbed their contents avidly. They had a more mature style than the other comics, contained no cartoons, had mystery stories and war yarns instead; the latter always saw the Germans getting the worst of it. They also were written with a better narrative and range of English than those of our former choosing. Bob Grogan, Eric Day and I came to an arrangement whereby we each chose one of these publications and asked our parents to send only the one of our choice. Eric also asked for the Champion. So, as they arrived we shared them between us and then discussed excitedly the stories afterwards and were impatient for the next issues. "V for Vengeance" was perhaps our favourite series, having an exciting realism whereas some others such as adventures of "Rockfist Rogan, RAF", sometimes reached too far into the realms of fantasy. His life-style seemed to often be like this. After a hectic day of shooting down several German aircraft he would arrive back in time that same evening to give the RAF station's bully a good hiding in the camp's boxing ring. Even so, we thoroughly enjoyed all these yarns as they fired our imaginations.

Sometime in the early months of 1940 Mr. King and his family left, presumably he was called up to the armed forces. His departure was unannounced and I was sorry to know that he had gone. His replacement was a woman, Miss Tinker, who occupied the vacated schoolhouse. She was in her twenties and at first seemed pleasant but soon proved to be the opposite. With her arrival the infant pupils moved into our classroom with a local assistant teacher, Mrs. Hawk, and we moved into the large one with the older village boys and girls. Miss Tinker soon made it clear that she was an ardent Communist and harangued us fairly frequently about the benefits of the Soviet system as perceived by her. She also informed we pupils were the, "The scum of the earth", an announcement that immediately alienated us from her. Though she did not use a cane as a punishment aid, she employed instead a heavy smack around the face of a boy that she thought had transgressed. It seemed that she rather enjoyed meting out this punishment and as she was of a stocky build, she had strength to go with it. We developed a sixth sense when a blow was coming but she had an answer to it. When we ducked under the first swing of her hand, she caught us with a backhand as we rose. Her knuckles stung even more than her palm. Her colleague, Mrs. Hawk, was also a nasty individual and one who should never have been entrusted with pupils. She had a permanently sour expression on her face as though she was chewing a wasp and her general demeanour was one of dissatisfaction. She also had a technique of ingratiating herself with the senior teacher by some ostensibly kindly act thereby artfully using it later as a means to influence her senior's opinions and attitudes towards pupils.

It was during Miss Tinker's time in 1941 that I sat the eleven plus examination that would determine whether or not I would advance to Grammar School. On the day of the examination all candidates were seated at one end of in the main classroom with non-candidates at the other. Major Royle supervised us jointly with Miss Tinker by standing at the front of the class. I think four papers were set for us being; respectively, English, English Composition and two of Arithmetic, a thirty-minute period was allowed for each paper. The time to stop work on a paper was announced by Miss Tinker at the end of each period. I seemed to be going well and having reached the first paper set for arithmetic I became engrossed in it. Concentrating hard, I became oblivious to all else around me. We had been told that should we finish a paper before time was up, we were to wait with arms folded until given permission to start on the next. Having finished the first of the arithmetic papers I sat as told but shortly after felt uneasy, as my fellow examinees were still busy writing. I caught Bob Grogan's eye and tried to ask him by gestures if he had started on the second paper. He did not understand me. A call from Miss Tinker demanded what I was doing to which I asked if I should have started on the second paper. "Yes", she said looking surprised and turning to the Major asked, "Do you think that boy was cheating?" Looking startled, The Major said brusquely, "No, I think not".

With the news that I was late in starting the paper I broke out in a sweat and in a panic got on with it. As there were only about ten to fifteen minutes left I could only attempt a few of the problems set and it was then all over. When the results came through only one evacuee, Herbert Herbert, had passed for grammar school, the rest had failed. A week or so later Frank and I were told that we were to go to Park Modern Secondary School as we had passed but at a lower level of attainment than that for grammar school. Though a second best, that seemed better than nothing but required us to leave Shapwick to attend our new school that had been evacuated to a part of Somerset distant from the village. My mum and dad were delighted with my success at this somewhat lower level, especially my dad. Before long they had sent a grey suit to me, it being the required uniform for the school. My mum and dad then came to see me and stayed at the farmhouse for a few days. Dad asked me if I was happy there and I replied, "Yes," which was the truth. He and Mum discussed this in the light of my possible departure and asked of Mr. and Mrs. Stevens if they were willing to keep me with them as Mum and Dad did not wish to risk me finding myself billeted elsewhere where I might be unhappy. They agreed and so I stayed in Shapwick. Frank left for his new school and I only saw him once more when I was in my early twenties on a chance meeting in Dagenham. He had joined the RAF.

As in many schools in those days various tasks were allocated to some of the older pupils other that the usual lessons. One that I among others was given on a rota was that of milk monitor. In contrast to the bottled milk that we were given in the Dagenham School, at the village school milk was delivered in an un-bottled bulk sufficient for the needs of all children. As it was fresh from cows it had to be sterilized by boiling in a large saucepan set on the "slow but sure" Tortoise Stove. Miss Tinker herself kept an eye on this milk so that it did not boil over but just before our mid-morning break, the milk was poured into cups and distributed to all children. I enjoyed this little job because a thick creamy scum formed on top of the boiled milk, which I liked, so was able to claim it for myself. When it was almost time to leave for our mid-day meal the cups and saucepan had to be washed by the monitor of the day. Miss Tinker and Mrs. Hawk marvelled at the way I got them clean without benefit of soap powder in the hot water. I smiled and kept quiet for if they had inspected the saucepan and cups a little more closely they would have found they had a slightly greasy film within, but no one fell sick from it.

Miss Tinker stayed for about a year by which time a number of evacuees had drifted home to London either because their parents thought that things there were relatively safe or they had reached school leaving age. With more children advancing to junior ages from the infants class the older children both local and evacuees, including girls, were transferred to Mr. Berry's class at the village hall. He was a tall, elderly, grey old-fashioned man with a slight stoop with a long ponderous stride. He embellished his stride with a walking stick that he used in an exaggerated way to keep pace. He lived with his wife in part of a thatched cottage, (the oldest cottage in the village) at one end of a short lane crossed by a stream with a ford, the hall being at the other. Instead of a school playground we used this metalled lane as a substitute. It was lined with willow trees and partway along, the stream and ford divided it. The passage of our running feet on the lane's grassy margins turned them into a layer of fine dust in dry weather and mud in wet. The boys played the usual football and other games but with warplanes in mind we also pretended to be aircraft on missions rushing about with arms outstretched and making engine noises. Then someone hit on an idea in imitation of a plane being shot down, so gathering dust in each hand he rushed along releasing streams of dust in simulation of smoke from engines on fire. Soon we were all at it and this game went on intermittently for two or three weeks. It was banned when Mr. Berry noticed that not only were we returning to class in a dusty state, the girls and several of the smaller boys arrived coughing repeatedly.

The stream and ford was also the focus of our attention and fantasies. Boys like to throw stones in water merely for the splash but we took this to a higher plane. Having had our heads filled with stories of the Spanish Armada in our history lessons we had Armada battles. Floating several twigs down-stream in representation of ships, they came under heavy bombardment from showers of stones and rocks aimed at them. It was all exciting and satisfying except when one of the twigs escaped to float off downstream out of range without being blown out of the water as we did not want any Spaniards to escape. Standing to throw stones from both banks we all got well splashed with water and returned to our lessons smelling of damp and algae.

Mr. Berry had a strong belief in the liberal use of the cane on boys but had a gentle, smiling attitude towards the girls. As a pianist he loved classical music and tried to drum into our heads the same feeling for it through the works of Schubert, Brahms and Chopin. He and his wife, who was a violinist, gave occasional duet recitals at Bridgwater that were later reported in the "Bridgwater Mercury". From this newspaper's announcements we learnt that his first names were Frank and George, which we called him behind his back. He also gave us two singing lessons each day at the hall and sometimes three, which we thought, was overdoing things, feeling that even two lessons were too much. As we became more and more tired of singing lessons we boys decided to rile him by singing off key. We did this by successive individual efforts so the position of the off key sound varied in direction. Mr. Berry usually stood at the front of the class waving his arms to keep time in the traditional way. However when he heard a groaning sound he began to head in its direction, head cocked on one side and in a semi crouch as though stalking. Approaching the source of the groaning, the culprit's voice changed to a boyish soprano and his face took on a look of angelic innocence. Almost at once, groaning commenced from elsewhere. We did this a little at first so not to rile him too much but during one lesson we went too far as we had him almost scampering about, listening intently. Calling to us to stop singing, in a towering rage he snarled that the whole class would resume the lesson at noon being the time we ordinarily left the hall to return home for our midday meal. Moreover we were to stay and sing until he was entirely satisfied with our performance. At noon for about the following fifteen to twenty minutes, we all sang sweetly and, still rattled, he then dismissed us. We didn't try that jape again but we enjoyed it at the time.

32 Mr Berry's cottage

He also had a militaristic attitude and on one day each week, marched the older boys in a double file up and down the street outside the hall barking orders, "Left right, left right, left turn, right turn, about turn", etc. He was preparing us for military service but we only thought of it as a release from our lessons. He also developed a cunning technique to get us boys to confess to misdemeanours. If some mischief had occurred he would ask the culprits to stand. If no-one did, he then adapted a sneering tone of contempt saying, "I had not known that this class had among its pupils some dirty Germans". This was too much to bear for the boys so the wrongdoers stood and accepted their punishment. One matter that he was also keen on was sketch drawing in which I was very interested. Drawing lessons usually took place once each week and some children hated it but a few others and I loved it. We often had to copy a picture such as a stagecoach and four from a Christmas card or similar. Sometimes we had free choice when we could use our imaginations for a subject. He also taught us a little about perspective and required us to draw a large shiny ball or jug to capture by shading, its "round appearance" using those actual words and indicating roundness by shaping his hands. He used "round appearance" so frequently that it became a term we copied in amused derision about him when out of his hearing. Even so, I found this exercise very useful and often had the honour of having drawings pinned and displayed on the wall. There was one boy from West Ham who had the edge over me as his drawings had a fluidity that I could not quite match.

The cane was administered at least once each week to one boy or another for misdemeanours, myself taking a share. One day when told to hold out my hand for this punishment I defied him because I thought it unfair and in a rage he snatched at my arm swung me around and gave five or six strokes to my backside. He ordered me out and into the cloakroom where he made me kneel as he stood over me threateningly with the cane. After a lecture from him we then returned to the class and the lesson. When it was playtime break, Mr. Berry told me to stay as the others left and that I was to go into the storeroom and he would follow shortly. When he arrived he told me to take down my shorts so he could inspect my bottom. I did not want to do that so said that the marks could be seen if I pulled up the hem which I did. Studying his handiwork for a few seconds he told me to go off to the playtime break. When I arrived my mates gathered around me asking how I was. By rolling up the hem of my shorts again I displayed a few of the red weals on my left buttock. Though they were sore I basked in the admiration of these boys and though I had been given a fright, I hadn't cried. Looking back I think that this teacher had a few qualms about what he had done and became a little more restrained in his use of the cane thereafter.

The bombing of Bristol caused a further influx of evacuees to Shapwick but comprised only a few children. Among them were a brother and sister, he about seven and she thirteen. She was in fact a strong-looking well-developed young woman. The other pupils received her and her brother in a natural and friendly manner as they joined us in Mr. Berry's class. One morning after a week or so, brother and sister were sent to wait in the cloakroom until called, the girl leaving the class scarlet-faced under the gaze of the rest of the pupils. When gone, Mr. Berry told us that we should treat them in a friendly way and should not comment upon their appearance. I suppose that some of the older girls knew what he was driving at but the rest of us were baffled as to his meaning. The only thing different about the girl was that she had an unusual hairstyle it being uniformly short. The two were then recalled to their desks with the girl still red-faced with embarrassment. Later in the playground the boys wondered about this mystery until a village girl said that at Bristol, both had lice ridden hair which had been shaved off hence its shortness. Up until then we had just accepted her as she was but the insensitive and ham-fisted approach to the subject by the teacher deeply hurt the girl and highlighted the problem she had suffered. We realised that brother and sister had been living in crowded public shelters during the bombing and had probably become infested at that time through no fault of their own. Poor kids!

As had happened with many Dagenham boys and for similar reasons, those from West Ham began to drift home to London so the class size at the hall gradually got smaller. One boy played a prank on Mr. Berry on his last Saturday in the village (he was the one who was my rival in art and possessed of a good sense of humour). In chalk on the hall door he wrote, "Shapwick Constipation Camp, Commandant Frank George Berry" in a parody of a German concentration camp. On the following Monday when unlocking the door, Mr. Berry was very annoyed when his eyes met this message. Early in our lessons, he instructed a pupil to erase from the door the offending message. He then ordered each individual pupil to write his/her name at the top of a sheet of paper followed by his lower down for him to collect when all had finished. Every child present knew all of his names and had to contemplate how straightforward they were going to be in their response. The girls mostly wrote "Mr. Berry"; the boys came up with the same but others wrote either, "F. G. Berry" or "Frank Berry" the latter being by a further few and me. Nobody wrote the full version. He studied these sheets after collection but remained mystified. He asked how some pupils knew his initials or his first name but we were ready for that and merely said we had seen the reports in the local newspaper. Nothing further was said until the week had almost passed. Then in a ruminative way he said to some of us boys, "I wonder if the boy who left was the one who wrote on the door". He wasn't as daft as we had begun to think so we hastened to tell a fib claiming that the boy had left on the Friday evening so that was the end of the matter. We weren't going to let down our departed friend. That episode seemed to signal the end of our class at the village hall as Mr. and Mrs. Berry soon left and we reduced number of his pupils returned to lessons at the village school proper.

Back at that school a woman was the new senior teacher. She had a much gentler approach in controlling us and we rather liked her so she and we got along well. Her time with us was a relatively happy one except that the evil Mrs. Hawk was still there. Once again she had gained her usual influence by way of ingratiating herself with her senior colleague. One of our lessons each week was on handicrafts. We were given some stiff, small mesh netting and told to make a groceries type shopping bag by weaving strands of coloured raffia in the mesh to make a pattern. We could buy the finished articles if we wished. The class enjoyed doing this work; with mine having a colourful zigzag design. I had got about one third of it done at a time when Mrs. Hawk was in the room talking to her colleague. She then decided to visit the pupils to see their progress. Arriving at my desk she said, "I like that. I would like to buy it when it is finished". "I replied, "I am sorry but I am making it for my mum". I could tell that this was not good news to her. This once per week lesson continued for about a month until one day at the beginning of the lesson, I discovered that my work had vanished from the workbag hanging on the front of my desk. I raised a hand to gain the teacher's attention and it so happened that Mrs. Hawk was again present. I was asked what I wanted? I answered that my work had gone and was told I should look for it more thoroughly. This I did but without success and reported its absence to the senior teacher. I was told that I had been careless and Mrs. Hawk joined in, saying that I should learn not to be so negligent with my things. I was expecting the rest of the class to be asked to look in their workbags but none were. I had the feeling that something was odd for in other similar circumstances all children would have been told to search their workbags. I sat down mystified but nothing more was said about it and Mum would not have my present after all. However, many weeks later, my friend Bob Grogan, was told to go to Mrs. Hawk's classroom to fetch an item from her cupboard which he did. Later in the playground he told me that my raffia work was hidden there at the rear of the bottom shelf. In the circumstances, it seemed to me that she had stolen it from me. I wondered later if it had ever been completed.

Another small incident that concerned Mrs. Hawk arose over a large drawing in chalk on the road at the village cross roads. It was of a cowboy in traditional cowboy clothes and there was nothing offensive about it and could only be seen when near. Riding her bicycle to school from Ashcott, Mrs. Hawk saw it and took on an attitude of outrage. At assembly that morning with the senior teacher present she demanded to know the culprit and a boy duly owned up. We were then asked if anyone else had helped to draw it. No one had but some of us were not going to let our friend come in for punishment alone. Three or four of us boys put up our hands and claimed to have added the cowboy's gun, his scarf, badge and spurs even though our confessions were untruthful. This diluted the ire directed at the artist and after a few scornful remarks from Mrs. Hawk the culprit was sent with a bucket and broom to wash away the offending picture.

In the final year of my stay in the village yet another teacher arrived to take charge to live in the schoolhouse. She was Mrs. Cook, a kindly, motherly woman who treated us well. Her husband was pleasant, small and of a very slight build. Seemingly unfit for work he remained unemployed for months. So, once more we resumed our lessons in this the happiest stage of our school life since the time of Mr. King. Mrs. Hawk seemed not to have the influence she once enjoyed but unfortunately for succeeding pupils, remained in post for years after. A few weeks before the summer break, we boys who were due to leave that year were allocated less classroom work. Instead we found that we were given practical work in the rather overgrown schoolhouse back garden. This we dug, weeded, mowed and generally tidied, chatting in a relaxed way together and with only a little larking about. We thought that because of his obvious physical weakness, the work that we were doing was too heavy for the teacher's husband and I must say that we enjoyed doing it and the sense of freedom that it gave. I suppose our teacher had killed two birds with one stone with this ploy. She got us from under her feet and a tidy garden at no cost.

My companions being slightly older than me left for Dagenham or West Ham and their homes at the start of the school summer holiday. This was when I began to feel lonely and unhappy as few schoolmates of my age remained and those that did, lived at farms outlying from the village. I returned to school in September for a few weeks until my birthday in October. Dad had asked Mr. and Mrs. Stevens if there was a chance that I could remain with them and work on the farm. Mum and Dad still wanted me safe from harm as bombing of London continued though at a much less intensity and rather sporadically.

33 Many children drifted back to the cities

To stay was not possible, as the farm could not support another worker not least because Norman was to soon leave his grammar school at Street to work with his father. Moreover I had become rather rebellious and my departure was, no doubt, a release and relief for Mrs. Stevens. My dad came to collect me, including my pet rabbit, my clothes, etc, and. so we said goodbye. Carrying the rabbit in a large, closed cardboard box, Dad and I boarded a Bristol Blue bus for Bridgwater, then a train for London. Glad though I was to be returning home to my family I knew that I would miss the Stevens family, the farm and village life. It also crossed my mind as to whether I would survive the German attacks on London that were soon to enter another dangerous phase from flying bombs and rockets.

32 EPILOGUE

When I returned home to Dagenham and to Mum, Dad and Grandad, as I entered the living room for the first time in four years, there on the chimney breast was a paper banner which said, "Welcome home Ted". It pleased me very much and even more that, it was kept in place for a few days. Our home seemed to have shrunk since I had left, particularly when compared with the spaciousness of Old Farm. Every room seemed very small but I soon got used to it. It was a great comfort to be with Mum and Dad as I felt that I was with people who loved me and whom I loved in return. Though I had been well looked after by Mr. and Mrs. Stevens, I knew that I was, in effect, an intruder in their home and family, a situation that I could understand from their point of view. For the first few weeks after my arrival I had little wish to go out but was happy to be in the security in my real family. My sisters were absent as Minnie was conscripted into the army, serving in the ATS (the Auxiliary Territorial Service) in an anti-aircraft unit. Rosemary was in Gloucestershire to where she had been evacuated with the company for whom she worked. I soon met my pals with whom I had been at school with before the war and we continued as friends as we had then and going around together.

It would be true to say that there were times when I missed the country life that I had known. Dagenham seemed rather drab which had a lot to do with the privations that three years of war had brought and though one could not tell, it was only halfway through. Moreover, compared with Shapwick the air was dirty and our garden and its plants all carried a dusting of soot. It reminded me of Jack Exon's term when meeting me, "Hello Lunnon, be you down from the smoake". These thoughts caused me to express them to my sister Minnie a few times to which she retorted, "Well, if you miss Shapwick so much, you had better go back there". I suppose that I deserved what she said but it had the effect of curbing my tongue on the subject. I did write back to Mr. and Mrs. Stevens to say that we had got home safely and to thank them for all that they had done for me. At the time I did not know that this was the start of an intermittent correspondence and other contacts with their family that continued for years up to and beyond the death of Mrs. Stevens at the age of almost one hundred and three years.

34 A visit to Mrs Stevens and Marjorie during my National Service

This keeping in touch developed further from correspondence. At about the age of seventeen I asked if I could visit the family at Old Farm to which they agreed. It was good to see them again and Marjorie had grown beyond the early toddler stage and she and I got on well together. I also went with Norman to a dance at which there was a country style band where we had a great time to the music and meeting girls. In 1949 when I was in the Royal Navy doing National Service and stationed at Devonport I paid another visit for a weekend whilst in my sailor's uniform. This caused a surprise, not least to Granny Moxey who seemed to like it. Sadly through ill health, she was bedridden and I met her, as she lay in her bed in her usual bedroom up the narrow stairs in the ancient part of the farmhouse.

35 A weekend visit in 1949

Ten more years passed when Jean Thomas and I married and as part of our honeymoon we stayed a week with the Stevens family again. Their hospitality was as generous as ever and what was really touching, Mr. and Mrs. Stevens in honour of our newly wedded state gave up their own bed to us during our stay. Other occasional visits continued over the years including with our daughters when they were young. Once or twice my mum and dad also paid happy visits when they too were generously received.

As the years progressed and, as would be expected, changes took place. Mr. Stevens reached retirement and though he and his wife wished to continue to live at Old Farm it was not to be. They moved to a bungalow in nearby Ashcott village and the Vesty Estate that to this day owns the village and its farms and woods, sold Old Farm and its orchard for housing development. It must have been a sad day for them and their family. Though the farmhouse remained as a private dwelling, the orchard where I had spent many a happy hour was cleared of its out buildings, apple trees and the two magnificent walnut trees. When I first saw these changes I too was very sad for gone was the colour and scent of Spring that came with the apple blossom. Though lost, it still remains in my mind as a cherished memory. It was replaced by a collection of individual dwellings, admittedly built to a high standard in keeping with the style of the local stone but, selfishly perhaps, I preferred it as it was. This was the first of many instances of a gradual in-filling of similar sites in the village with only the larger outlying farms remaining. The lovely Loxley oak wood with its glades and hazel bushes was almost clear-felled and close planted with conifers; another great loss in the thoughts of at least some local people but definitely myself. The great elms that lined parts of back lane also were felled for their valuable timber. These gave shade in the summer and included the one that I climbed as a boy and where I nearly got stuck neither able to go up nor down. With the advent of Dutch elm disease they would have later been lost so their passing was inevitable in the long term. Happy Harry's carpentry and joiner's workshop had now been converted to a dwelling. Performed by his sons and a grandson, here many different skills were seen including one that I now think is rare, that of a wheelwright. These abilities and those of the village blacksmith and farmers kept this small community mostly self-sufficient.

Another great loss to the Stevens family and also to me was the death of Mr. Stevens at the early age of seventy-three of a heart attack. He was enjoying his retirement, socialising and playing bowls at a club in Bridgwater and it was a great pity that these days for him did not last very long. He was a popular and well-known figure in Shapwick and other surrounding villages. I was invited to attend his funeral at Shapwick Church and testament to his popularity was the standing room only attendance in the congregation. He did not replace my father but he was a man I much admired and respected and with whom I had spent many a happy hour.

36 Alice Stevens with me and my wife Jean.

So the years passed and still I was able to frequently return to visit and stay for several days with Norman and Dulcie Stevens. As I have earlier said, they too became very successful farmers at New Farm. I will never forget one day being asked by another baffled farmer from a nearby village how did Norman do it. I replied in the gentlest way that I could that it was because he was a highly intelligent man could think and plan ahead. Alas, the day came when he too died and once more the attendance at the church for his funeral was again, standing room only. I cannot say how he felt about me but I came to regard him as the brother I never had. Upon Mrs. Stevens reaching her hundredth birthday, a hall was hired in Ashcott where a buffet was provided for the stream of visitors and well-wishers that came to see this lady on her great day.

Lifetime of hard work pays off for Alice on her 100th birthday

AN Ashcott woman was overwhelmed with surprises during her 100th birthday celebrations.

Alice Stevens turned 100 years young on September 19, and to mark the occasion a party was held for 50 friends and famil[y] at the village hall.

Mrs Stevens was overwhelmed with flowers, gifts and cards, including a special birthday message from Her Majesty the Queen.

But to top off her big day she was delighted to receive a surprise visit from Ted Baverstock, who, as a child, was evacuated to her home during the Second World War.

She also celebrated the day with her daughter, Marjorie Bessant, two grandchildren and six great-grandchildren.

Marjorie said: "My mum really enjoyed seeing everyone at the party, and would like to thank everyone who came and for all of the lovely gifts."

"Ted popped down with his wife, Jean."

When she was asked what the secret of her mum's longevity could possibly be Marjorie said: "Mum's a quiet woman and has played an active part in the church, but she is a bit of a worrier.

"She doesn't smoke or drink and has worked hard all her life."

37 Alice Stevens on her 100th birthday (photo and article reprinted by kind permission of the Bridgwater Mercury)

This was yet another tribute to both her and her family. Inevitably considering her age, almost three years later she too died having just entered hospital. My wife Jean and I attended her funeral and again, a packed congregation.

38 Dulcie, Norman and my wife Jean

Dulcie remains to this day a true friend and I am regularly in touch with her and occasionally some others of the family. During our last visit in 2010, I once more wandered the lanes and byways of the village, meeting some of those that I knew from the past. In my mind's eye I also saw the ghosts of others that once I romped and roamed with in the fields and woods and also the horses and cows I worked with and the wild creatures I saw. The mediaeval Manor House was now a private school, the Elizabethan Shapwick House an hotel and the Old Vicarage a private house. The new in-fill houses now largely occupied by incomers many seemingly commuters to places like Bristol or Taunton. A highlight was when I called at Old Farm. There, I explained to the owners and their children, a girl and boy, who I was and that I had lived there as an evacuee upon which I was invited in where great changes were being wrought to the interior in the form of beautiful modernisation. I told them how its layout was when a farmhouse and they seemed very interested.

Characters like Jack Exon, The Major and many more that I knew now rested in the village churchyard. Here rank or wealth made no distinction, reminding me of an epitaph I once read. It was on the small headstone of an ordinary man and read,

"Here I lie by the Vestry door,

I lie here because I'm poor;

The further in the more you pay,

But I lie here as warm as they." A few words that caused me to think.

It seems that they, the village and its people had entered my very being and it was always a pleasure to return. I think that I saw the village and its people at the last stage between the change from late Victorian/ Edwardian life and traditions to the change to full agricultural mechanisation and, eventually, factory farming. Because age and other factors have to be considered, I doubt if Jean and I will ever return there. What I do know and have realised for some long time is, that I was extremely fortunate to have been billeted with the Stevens family, an experience that influenced me and changed some elements of my outlook on life for the better. The debt that I owe them can never be repaid but perhaps in some small way what I have written in these pages shows how deeply their many acts of friendship and generosity are appreciated

39 Class of '39

Back row: Herbert Herbert, Len Wallace, Harry Stodart, Sid Stodart, Donald Rutherford

Second row: Bob Grogan, Brian Turnbull, Ted Baverstock, Unknown, 'Daddy' Christmas

Third row: Frank Crann, Unknown twin brothers

Front row: Douglas Rutherford, Brian Prill, Albert, Ron Prill, Peter Prill

Classroom Assistant: Teenage girl believed to be from the village.

33. GLOSSARY

Imperial and metric weights and measures

(near approximations)

1 inch	= 25 millimetres
1 foot = 12 inches	= 0.30 metre
1 yard = 3 feet	= 0.91 metre
1 mile = 1,760 yards	= 1.609 kilometres
1 acre = 4,840 square yards	= 0.405 hectares
10 acres	= 4 hectares
1 pound = 16 ounces	= 0.45 kilogram
1 hundredweight	= 51 kilograms
1 pint	= 0.56 litre
1 gallon = 4 pints	= 4.5 litres

Made in United States
Troutdale, OR
07/18/2024